Test Yourself

Developmental Psychology

Test Yourself... Psychology Series

Test Yourself: Biological Psychology ISBN 978 0 85725 649 2

Test Yourself: Cognitive Psychology ISBN 978 0 85725 669 0

Test Yourself: Developmental Psychology ISBN 978 0 85725 657 7

Test Yourself: Personality and Individual Differences ISBN 978 0 85725 661 4

Test Yourself: Research Methods and Design in Psychology ISBN 978 0 85725 665 2

Test Yourself: Social Psychology ISBN 978 0 85725 653 9

Test Yourself

Developmental Psychology

Dominic Upton and Penney Upton

Multiple-Choice Questions prepared by Charlotte Taylor

LearningMatters

First published in 2011 by Learning Matters Ltd

British Library Cataloguing in Publication Data
A CIP record for this book is available from the British Library

ISBN: 978 0 85725 657 7

This book is also available in the following e-book formats:
Adobe ebook ISBN: 978 085725 659 1
ePUB book ISBN: 978 085725 658 4
Kindle ISBN: 978 0 85725 660 7

Cover design by Toucan Design
Text design by Toucan Design
Project Management by Deer Park Productions, Tavistock, Devon
Typeset by Pantek Media, Maidstone, Kent
Printed and bound in Great Britain by Bell & Bain Ltd, Glasgow

Learning Matters Ltd
20 Cathedral Yard
Exeter
EX1 1HB
Tel: 01392 215560
info@learningmatters.co.uk
www.learningmatters.co.uk

Contents

Acknowledgements

The production of this series has been a rapid process with an apparent deadline at almost every turn. We are therefore grateful to colleagues both from Learning Matters (Julia Morris and Helen Fairlie) and the University of Worcester for making this process so smooth and (relatively) effortless. In particular we wish to thank our colleagues for providing many of the questions, specifically:

- Biological Psychology: Emma Preece
- Cognitive Psychology: Emma Preece
- Developmental Psychology: Charlotte Taylor
- Personality and Individual Differences: Daniel Kay
- Research Methods and Design in Psychology: Laura Scurlock-Evans
- Social Psychology: Laura Scurlock-Evans

Finally, we must, once again, thank our children (Gabriel, Rosie and Francesca) for not being as demanding as usual during the process of writing and development.

Introduction

Psychology is one of the most exciting subjects that you can study at university in the twenty-first century. A degree in psychology helps you to understand and explain thought, emotion and behaviour. You can then apply this knowledge to a range of issues in everyday life including health and well-being, performance in the workplace, education – in fact any aspect of life you can think of! However, a degree in psychology gives you much more than a set of 'facts' about mind and behaviour; it will also equip you with a wide range of skills and knowledge. Some of these, such as critical thinking and essay writing, have much in common with humanities subjects, while others such as hypothesis testing and numeracy are scientific in nature. This broad-based skill set prepares you exceptionally well for the workplace – whether or not your chosen profession is in psychology. Indeed, recent evidence suggests employers appreciate the skills and knowledge of psychology graduates. A psychology degree really can help you get ahead of the crowd. However, in order to reach this position of excellence, you need to develop your skills and knowledge fully and ensure you complete your degree to your highest ability.

This book is designed to enable you, as a psychology student, to maximise your learning potential by assessing your level of understanding and your confidence and competence in developmental psychology, one of the core knowledge domains for psychology. It does this by providing you with essential practice in the types of questions you will encounter in your formal university assessments. It will also help you make sense of your results and identify your strengths and weaknesses. This book is one part of a series of books designed to assist you with learning and developing your knowledge of psychology. The series includes books on:

- Biological Psychology
- Cognitive Psychology
- Developmental Psychology
- Personality and Individual Differences
- Research Methods and Design in Psychology
- Social Psychology

In order to support your learning this book includes over 200 targeted Multiple-Choice Questions (MCQs) and Extended Multiple-Choice Questions (EMCQs) that have been carefully put together to help assess your depth of knowledge of developmental psychology. The MCQs are split into two formats: the foundation level questions are about your level of understanding of the key principles and components of key areas in psychology. Hopefully, within these questions you should recognise the correct answer from the four options. The advanced level questions require more than simple recognition – some will require recall of key information, some will require application of this information and others will require synthesis of information. At the end of each chapter you will find a set of essay questions covering each of the topics. These are typical of the kinds of question that you are likely to encounter during your studies. In each chapter, the first essay question is broken down for you using a concept map, which is intended to help you develop a detailed answer to the question. Each of the concept maps is shaded to show you how topics link together, and includes cross-references to relevant MCQs in the chapter. You should be able to see a progression in your learning from the foundation to the advanced MCQs, to the extended MCQs and finally the essay questions. The book is divided up into 11 chapters and your developmental psychology module is likely to have been divided into similar topic areas. However, do not let this restrict your thinking in relation to developmental psychology: these topics interact. The sample essay questions, which complement the questions provided in the chapter, will help you to make the links between different topic areas. You will find the answers to all of the MCQs and EMCQs at the end of the book. There is a separate table of answers for each chapter; use the self monitoring column in each of the tables to write down your own results, coding correct answers as NC, incorrect answers as NI and any you did not respond to as NR. You can then use the table on page 113 to analyse your results.

The aim of the book is not only to help you revise for your exams, it is also intended to help with your learning. However, it is not intended to replace lectures, seminars and tutorials, or to supersede the book chapters and journal articles signposted by your lecturers. What this book can do, however, is set you off on a sound footing for your revision and preparation for your exams. In order to help you to consolidate your learning, the book also contains tips on how to approach MCQ assessments and how you can use the material in this text to assess, *and enhance*, your knowledge base and level of understanding.

Now you know the reasons behind this book and how it will enhance your success, it is time for you to move on to the questions – let the fun begin!

Assessing your interest, competence and confidence

The aim of this book is to help you to maximise your learning potential by assessing your level of understanding, confidence and competence in core issues in psychology. So how does it do this?

Assessing someone's knowledge of a subject through MCQs might at first glance seem fairly straightforward: typically the MCQ consists of a question, one correct answer and one or more incorrect answers, sometimes called distractors. For example, in this book each question has one right answer and three distractors. The goal of an MCQ test is for you to get every question right and so show just how much knowledge you have. However, because you are given a number of answers to select from, you might be able to choose the right answer either by guessing or by a simple process of elimination – in other words by knowing what is not the right answer. For this reason it is sometimes argued that MCQs only test knowledge of facts rather than in-depth understanding of a subject. However, there is increasing evidence that MCQs can also be valuable at a much higher level of learning, if used in the right way (see, for example, Gardner-Medwin and Gahan, 2003). They can help you to develop as a self-reflective learner who is able to recognise the interest you have in a subject matter as well as your level of competence and confidence in your own knowledge.

MCQs can help you gauge your interest, competence and confidence in the following way. It has been suggested (Howell, 1982) that there are four possible states of knowledge (see Table 1). Firstly, it is possible that you do not know something and are not aware of this lack of knowledge. This describes the naive learner – think back to your first week at university when you were a 'fresher' student and had not yet begun your psychology course. Even if you had done psychology at A level, you were probably feeling a little self-conscious and uncertain in this new learning environment. During the first encounter in a new learning situation most of us feel tentative and unsure of ourselves; this is because we don't yet know what it is we don't know – although to feel this lack of certainty suggests that we know there is something we don't know, even if we don't yet know what this is! In contrast, some people appear to be confident and at ease even in new learning situations; this is not usually because they already know everything but rather because they too do not yet know what it is they do not know – but they have yet to even acknowledge that there is a gap in their knowledge. The next step on from this 'unconscious non-competence' is 'conscious non-competence'; once you started your psychology course you began to realise what the gaps were in your knowledge – you now knew what you didn't know! While this can be an uncomfortable feeling, it is important for the learning process that this acknowledgement of a gap in knowledge is made, because it is the first step in reaching the next level of learning – that of a 'conscious competent' learner. In other words you need to know what the gap in your knowledge is so that you can fill it.

Table 1 Consciousness and competence in learning

	Unconscious	Conscious
Non-competent	You don't know something and are not aware that you lack this knowledge/skill.	You don't know something and are aware that you lack this knowledge/skill.
Competent	You know something but are not aware of your knowledge/ skill.	You know something and are aware of your knowledge/ skill.

One of the ways this book can help you move from unconscious non-competency to conscious competency should by now be clear – it can help you identify the gaps in your knowledge. However, if used properly it can do much more; it can also help you to assess your consciousness and competence in this knowledge.

When you answer an MCQ, you will no doubt have a feeling about how confident you are about your answer: 'I know the answer to question 1 is A. Question 2 I am not so sure about. I am certain the answer is not C or D, so it must be A or B. Question 3, I haven't got a clue so I will say D – but that is a complete guess.' Sound familiar? Some questions you know the answers to, you have that knowledge and know you have it; other questions you are less confident about but think you may know which (if not all) are the distractors, while for others you know this is something you just don't know. Making use of this feeling of confidence will help you become a more reflective – and therefore effective – learner.

Perhaps by now you are wondering where we are going with this and how any of this can help you learn. 'Surely all that matters is whether or not I get the answers right? Does that show I have knowledge?' Indeed it may well do and certainly, if you are confident in your answers, then yes it does. But what if you were not sure? What if your guess of D for our fictional question 3 above was correct? What if you were able to complete all the MCQs in a test and score enough to pass – but every single answer was a guess? Do you really know and understand psychology because you have performed well – and will you be able to do the same again if you retake the test next week? Take a look back at Table 1. If you are relying on guesswork and hit upon the answer by accident you might perform well without actually understanding how you know the answer, or that you even knew it (unconscious competence), or you may not realise you don't know something (unconscious non-competence). According to this approach to using

MCQs what is important is not how many answers you get right, but whether or not you acknowledge your confidence in the answer you give: it is better to get a wrong answer and acknowledge it is wrong (so as to work on filling that gap).

Therefore what we recommend you do when completing the MCQs is this: for each answer you give, think about how confident you are that it is right. You might want to rate each of your answers on the following scale:

3:    I am confident this is the right answer.

2:    I am not sure, but I think this is the right answer.

1:    I am not sure, but I think this is the wrong answer.

0:    I am confident this is the wrong answer.

Using this system of rating your confidence will help you learn for yourself both what you know and what you don't know. You will become a conscious learner through the self-directed activities contained in this book. Reflection reinforces the links between different areas of your learning and knowledge and strengthens your ability to *justify* an answer, so enabling you to perform to the best of your ability.

References

Gardner-Medwin, A.R. and Gahan, M. (2003) *Formative and Summative Confidence-Based Assessment*, Proceedings of 7th International Computer-Aided Assessment Conference, Loughborough, UK, July, pp. 147–55.

Howell, W.C. (1982) 'An overview of models, methods, and problems', in W.C. Howell and E.A. Fleishman (eds), *Human performance and productivity, Vol. 2: Information processing and decision making*. Hillsdale, NJ: Erlbaum.

Tips for success: how to succeed in your assessments

This book, part of a comprehensive new series, will help you achieve your psychology aspirations. It is designed to assess your knowledge so that you can review your current level of performance and where you need to spend more time and effort reviewing and revising material. However, it hopes to do more than this – it aims to assist you with your learning so it not only acts as an assessor of performance but as an aid to learning. Obviously, it is not a replacement for every single text, journal article, presentation and abstract you will read and review during the course of your degree programme. Similarly, it is in no way a replacement for your lectures, seminars or additional reading – it should complement all of this material. However, it will also add something to all of this other material: learning is assisted by reviewing and assessing and this is what this text aims to do – help you learn through assessing your learning.

The focus throughout this book, as it is in all of the books in this series, is on how you should approach and consider your topics in relation to assessment and exams. Various features have been included to help you build up your skills and knowledge ready for your assessments.

This book, and the other companion volumes in this series, should help you learn through testing and assessing yourself – it should provide an indication of how advanced your thinking and understanding is. Once you have assessed your understanding you can explore what you need to learn and how. However, hopefully, quite a bit of what you read here you will already have come across and the text will act as a reminder and set your mind at rest – you do know your material.

Succeeding at MCQs

Exams based on MCQs are becoming more and more frequently used in higher education and particularly in psychology. As such you need to know the best strategy for completing such assessments and succeeding. The first thing to note is, if you know the material then the questions will present no problems – so revise and understand your notes and back this up with in-depth review of material presented in textbooks, specialist materials and journal articles. However, once you have done this you need to look at the technique for answering multiple-choice questions and here are some tips for success:

1. Time yourself. The first important thing to note when you are sitting your examination is the time available to you for completing it. If you have, for example, an hour and a half to answer 100 multiple-choice questions this means you have 54 seconds to complete each question. This means that you have to read, interpret, think about and select one answer for a multiple-choice question in under a minute. This may seem impossible, but there are several things that you can do to use your time effectively.

2. Practise. By using the examples in this book, those given out in your courses, in class tests, or on the web you can become familiar with the format and wording of multiple-choice questions similar to those used in your exam. Another way of improving your chances is to set your own multiple-choice exams – try and think of some key questions and your four optional responses (including the correct one of course!). Try and think of optional distractors that are sensible and not completely obvious. You could, of course, swap questions with your peers – getting them to set some questions for you while you set some questions for them. Not only will this help you with your practice but you will also understand the format of MCQs and the principles underlying their construction – this will help you answer the questions when it comes to the real thing.

3. The rule of totality. Look out for words like 'never' and 'always' in multiple-choice questions. It is rare in psychology for any answer to be true in relation to these words of 'totality'. As we all know, psychology is a multi-modal subject that has multiple perspectives and conflicting views and so it is very unlikely that there will always be a 'never' or an 'always'. When you see these words, focus on them and consider them carefully. A caveat is, of course, sometimes never and always will appear in a question, but be careful of these words!

4. Multiple, multiple-choice answers. Some multiple-choice answers will contain statements such as 'both A and C' or 'all of the above' or 'none of these'. Do not be distracted by these choices. Multiple-choice questions have only one correct answer and do not ask for opinion or personal bias. Quickly go through each choice independently, crossing off the answers that you know are not true. If, after eliminating the incorrect responses, you think there is more than one correct answer, group your answers and see if one of the choices matches yours. If you believe only one answer is correct, do not be distracted by multiple-choice possibilities.

5. 'First guess is best' fallacy. There is a myth among those who take (or even write) MCQs that the 'first guess is best'. This piece of folklore is misleading: research (and psychologists love research) indicates that when people change their answers on an MCQ exam, about two-thirds of the time they go from wrong to right, showing that the first guess is often not the best. So, think about it and consider your answer – is it right? Remember, your first guess is not better than a result obtained through good, hard, step-by-step, conscious thinking that enables you to select the answer that you believe to be the best.

6. The rule of threes. One of the most helpful strategies for multiple-choice questions is a three-step process:

(i)   Read the question thoroughly but quickly. Concentrate on particular words such as 'due to' and 'because' or 'as a result of' and on words of totality such as 'never' or 'always' (although see rule 3 above).

(ii) Rather than going to the first answer you think is correct (see rule 5) eliminate the ones that you think are wrong one by one. While this may take more time, it is more likely to provide the correct answer. Furthermore, answer elimination may provide a clue to a misread answer you may have overlooked.

(iii) Reread the question, as if you were reading it for the first time. Now choose your answer from your remaining answers based on this rereading.

7. Examine carefully. Examine each of the questions carefully, particularly those that are very similar. It may be that exploring parts of the question will be useful – circle the parts that are different. It is possible that each of the alternatives will be very familiar and hence you must **understand the meaning** of each of the alternatives with respect to the context of the question. You can achieve this by studying for the test as though it will be a short-answer or essay test. Look for the level of **qualifying words**. Such words as *best, always, all, no, never, none, entirely, completely* suggest that a condition exists without exception. Items containing words that provide for some level of exception or qualification are: *often, usually, less, seldom, few, more* and *most* (and see rule 3). If you know that two or three of the options are correct, **'all of the above'** is a strong possibility.

8. Educated guesses. Never leave a question unanswered. If nothing looks familiar, pick the answer that seems most complete and contains the most information. Most of the time (if not all of the time!) the best way to answer a question is to know the answer! However, there may be times when you will not know the answer or will not really understand the question. There are three circumstances in which you should guess: when you are stuck, when you are running out of time, or both of these! Guessing strategies are always dependent on the scoring system used to mark the exam (see the section on MCQ scoring mechanisms). If the multiple-choice scoring system makes the odds of gaining points equal to the odds of having points deducted it does not pay to guess if you are unable to eliminate any of the answers. But the odds of improving your test score are in your favour if you can rule out even one of the answers. The odds in your favour increase as you rule out more answers in any one question. So, take account of the scoring mechanisms and then eliminate, move onwards and guess!

9. Revise and learn. Study carefully and learn your material. The best tip for success is always to learn the material. Use this book, use your material, use your time wisely but, most of all, use your brain!

Chapter 1
Themes, theories and key figures in developmental psychology

This chapter provides questions relating to key issues and debates within developmental psychology, theories of human development, influential figures within developmental psychology and the use of research methods in the study of development.

Select one of the possible answers for each question.

Foundation level questions

1. The scientific study of human development began with the work of which influential psychologist?

    A. Charles Darwin.

    B. G. Stanley Hall.

    C. Arnold Gesell.

    D. Alfred Binet.

    Your answer:

2. Starting school, being able to vote, and starting university are examples of what type of influences?

    A. History-graded influences.

    B. Age-graded influences.

    C. Non-normative influences.

    D. Social influences.

    Your answer:

3. Which of the following is not a level of Bronfenbrenner's ecological systems theory?

    A. Mesosystem.

    B. Macrosystem.

    C. Ecosystem.

    D. Exosystem.

Your answer: ☐

4. Which key figure in developmental psychology did not view the child as an 'active learner'?

    A. Jean Piaget.

    B. Sigmund Freud.

    C. Lev Vygotsky.

    D. Urie Bronfenbrenner.

Your answer: ☐

5. Which developmental theorist views the person as developing within a system of nested structures?

    A. Erikson.

    B. Piaget.

    C. Bronfenbrenner.

    D. Vygotsky.

Your answer: ☐

6. Which key figure in developmental psychology suggested that development must be understood in relation to the cultural context?

    A. Sigmund Freud.

    B. Erik Erikson.

    C. Jean Piaget.

    D. Albert Bandura.

Your answer: ☐

7. The oral, anal, phallic, latency and genital stages are part of which theory?

    A. Erikson's psychosocial theory.

    B. Vygotsky's sociocultural theory.

    C. Social learning theory.

    D. Freud's psychosexual theory.

Your answer: ☐

8. Information processing theory, the idea that development can be understood as a series of mental operations, is influenced by which branch of psychology?

    A. Social psychology.

    B. Biological psychology.

    C. Cognitive psychology.

    D. Individual differences.

Your answer: ☐

9. In which research design would a researcher study the same group of participants over a period of time?

    A. Longitudinal.

    B. Cross-sectional.

    C. Sequential.

    D. Experimental.

Your answer: ☐

10. Which of these research methods is not commonly used in developmental psychology?

    A. Naturalistic observation.

    B. Clinical interview.

    C. Computer simulation.

    D. Case study.

Your answer: ☐

Advanced level questions

11. Which of the following theories views development as both a continuous and a discontinuous process?

   A. Information processing and behaviourism.

   B. Sociocultural theory and lifespan perspective.

   C. Cognitive development theory and social learning theory.

   D. Lifespan perspective and psychoanalytic perspective.

Your answer:

12. What are the main principles of the lifespan view of development?

   A. Development is lifelong, multidimensional and multi-directional.

   B. Development is lifelong, continuous and mediated by social interaction.

   C. Development is plastic and influenced by biological, historical, social and cultural factors.

   D. Both A and C.

Your answer:

13. According to Erikson, industry versus inferiority occurs at what age?

   A. 6–11 years.

   B. 1–3 years.

   C. Adolescence.

   D. 3–6 years.

Your answer:

14. According to Erikson, lack of warmth and responsive care from a caregiver during the first year of life may result in what?

   A. Shame and doubt.

   B. Guilt.

   C. Isolation.

   D. Mistrust.

Your answer:

15. Tom is 17 years old and learning to drive. His instructor explains to Tom how to perform the parallel parking manoeuvre. Which theory best exemplifies the role of his instructor?

   A. Vygotsky's sociocultural theory.

   B. Bronfenbrenner's ecological systems theory.

   C. Piaget's cognitive development theory.

   D. Social learning theory.

Your answer: ☐

16. Which of the following is *not* a criticism of Piaget's theory of cognitive development?

   A. Children's performance on many Piagetian tasks can be improved with training.

   B. Piaget's theory fails to account for environmental influences.

   C. Cognitive development does not occur after adolescence.

   D. Piaget's theory fails to take into account social and cultural influences.

Your answer: ☐

17. A 'sensitive period' is a term used to refer to what?

   A. An optimal time for certain abilities or capacities to develop.

   B. A time in which an individual's development is particularly affected by environmental influences.

   C. A critical period of development.

   D. Both A and B.

Your answer: ☐

18. For what reason might a researcher choose a clinical interview over a structured interview?

   A. It provides an in-depth insight into the participant's world.

   B. It enables the researcher to be guided by the participant's responses.

   C. It allows comparison between the participant's responses.

   D. Both A and B.

Your answer: ☐

19. What ethical considerations should a researcher take into account when conducting research with children?

A. Parental consent.

B. Child assent.

C. Cognitive abilities of the child.

D. All of the above.

Your answer: ☐

20. A researcher is interested in studying the educational experiences of children in gypsy communities. Which of the following research methods would be the most suitable?

A. Ethnography.

B. Case study.

C. Clinical interview.

D. Naturalistic observation.

Your answer: ☐

Extended multiple-choice question

Complete the following paragraphs using the items listed opposite. Not all of the items will be needed and each item can only be used once.

The nature versus nurture or the _____ versus _____ argument is one of the most controversial debates in the history of psychology. Contemporary thought emphasises an interaction between genes and environmental influences. _____ suggested that neurological and psychological functions are intrinsically linked to each other: one drives the development of the other therefore it is impossible to differentiate the two. As a result, researchers have now questioned the extent to which this occurs by investigating how much of the _____ can be explained by genetics and how genetics and the environment interact. Variance is measured by _____ obtained from kinship studies which compare the characteristics of family members, for example intelligence. However, this provides no indication of how intelligence develops and ignores the context in which development occurs.

_____ and _____ are two methods that have attempted to explain how genetics and the environment impact upon development and emphasise the idea that development is affected by _____ .

_____ suggests that development is additionally affected by _____ , the number of enduring relationships and activities that the person has in their immediate environment. Heredity estimates only tell us what the environment is bringing to fruition, the non-realised _____ remains unknown. In other words, it is not possible to determine the extent to which development is influenced by genetics and the environment.

Optional items

A. Armstrong (2007)

B. Bronfenbrenner

C. environment

D. heredity

E. heritability estimates

F. variance

G. genetic-environmental correlations

H. genetic potential

I. multidimensional factors

J. multiple interacting forces

K. proximal processes

L. reaction range

M. social interactions

N. Vygotsky

Essay questions for Chapter 1

Once you have completed the MCQs above you are ready to tackle some essay questions. You might like to select three or four topics and make notes on them. One way of doing this is to create a concept map. The first question has been done for you and you can see how the knowledge required links to some of the MCQs in this chapter.

1. Critically discuss the extent to which development is always affected by nature and nurture.

2. Discuss the contributions of both historical and contemporary figures in developmental psychology to our understanding of human development.

3. Critically evaluate the contribution of psychoanalytic theories to our understanding of development.

4. Jean Piaget is regarded as a highly influential figure in the history of developmental psychology. Discuss how Piaget's theory responded to many of the criticisms of behaviourism.

5. Bronfenbrenner's ecological systems theory has been credited as the most complete explanation of human development. Critically analyse this claim with reference to other major theories of human development.

6. Explain how Vygotsky's sociocultural theory and Bronfenbrenner's ecological systems theory emphasise the idea of the active child.

7. Evaluate the extent to which the lifespan perspective has contributed towards our understanding of human development.

8. With reference to examples, critically evaluate three research methods commonly used in developmental psychology.

Chapter 1 essay question 1: concept map

Critically discuss the extent to which development is always affected by nature and nurture.

The concept map below provides an example of the topic areas that you might include when writing your essay. Remember that it is important to link your answers to other topic areas not covered in this chapter. Good answers to this question will draw upon examples from a range of topics in developmental psychology and discuss how these illustrate genetic-environmental influences.

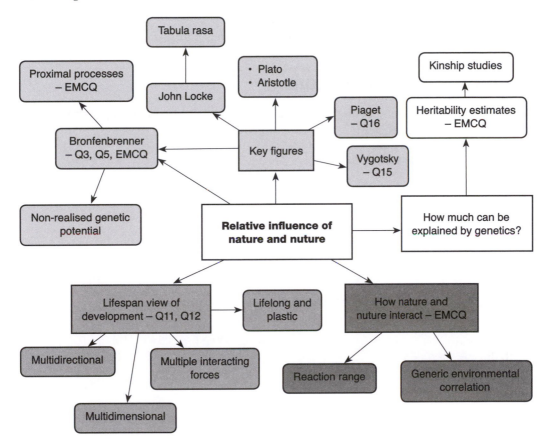

Chapter 2
Prenatal development and birth

This chapter provides questions relating to stages of prenatal development, factors influencing prenatal development, risks to typical prenatal development, prenatal learning and cognitive development and childbirth.

Select one of the possible answers for each question.

Foundation level questions

1. Complete the following sentence: prenatal development lasts for approximately _____ days beginning with _____ and ending with _____.

    A. 365, implantation, fertilisation.

    B. 266, fertilisation, birth.

    C. 240, conception, fertilisation.

    D. 195, implantation, birth.

    Your answer: ☐

2. Prenatal development can be divided into how many phases?

    A. 4.

    B. 5.

    C. 3.

    D. 6.

    Your answer: ☐

3. The first stage of prenatal development is known as the _____ period.

    A. Germinal.

    B. Embryonic.

    C. Foetal.

    D. Blastocyst.

    Your answer: ☐

4. The period of the zygote ends approximately how many weeks after conception?

    A. 1–2.

    B. 4.

    C. 3–4.

    D. 2.

Your answer: ☐

5. The three layers of the embryo are known as the endoderm, ectoderm and
_____?

    A. Mesoderm.

    B. Microderm.

    C. Macroderm.

    D. Exoderm.

Your answer: ☐

6. Facial features can be distinguished during which phase?

    A. Embryonic.

    B. Foetal.

    C. Germinal.

    D. Both A and B.

Your answer: ☐

7. The phenotype refers to what?

    A. An inherited trait.

    B. An observable trait.

    C. A trait subject to environmental influences.

    D. Both B and C.

Your answer: ☐

8. An agent that interferes with typical prenatal development is known as what?

   A. Teratogen.

   B. Villi.

   C. Phoneme.

   D. Genotype.

   Your answer: ☐

9. Illegal drug use during pregnancy has been linked to what?

   A. Low birth weight.

   B. Impaired motor development.

   C. Behavioural difficulties.

   D. All of the above.

   Your answer: ☐

10. Which of the following is the most vulnerable to harmful environmental factors?

    A. Embryo.

    B. Foetus.

    C. Blastocyst.

    D. Zygote.

    Your answer: ☐

Advanced level questions

11. Sophia contracted rubella during her third week of pregnancy. Which of the following may affect her newborn child?

    A. Low birth weight.

    B. Heart defects.

    C. Malformation of limbs.

    D. Pneumonia.

    Your answer: ☐

12. Anoxia, or inadequate oxygen supply during birth, may lead to what?

   A. Developmental disabilities, e.g. cerebral palsy.

   B. Irritability, but no long-lasting effects in mild cases.

   C. Problems in later development in both extreme and mild cases.

   D. Both A and B.

Your answer: ☐

13. Which of the following has prenatal learning not been linked to?

   A. Auditory perception.

   B. Exposure to teratogens.

   C. Increases in testosterone.

   D. Exposure to classical music.

Your answer: ☐

14. Research investigating prenatal learning has suggested that newborn infants can do what?

   A. Recognise music that they have been exposed to prenatally.

   B. Recognise speech patterns within their native language.

   C. Recognise their mother's voice.

   D. All of the above.

Your answer: ☐

15. Regardless of age, the risks of high maternal stress on prenatal development can be reduced by what?

   A. Seeking social support from friends and family.

   B. Taking vitamin supplements.

   C. Regular exercise over a six-month period.

   D. Drinking alcohol.

Your answer: ☐

16. Abigail decides to have an epidural to ease the pain of labour. What implications may her decision have for her newborn child?

A. Low birth weight, inattentiveness, anoxia.

B. Difficulty in feeding, increased sleepiness, longer labour.

C. Malnourishment, maternal tearing, feeding difficulties.

D. No potential for any harmful effects.

Your answer:

17. The increase in the number of Caesarean births worldwide over the past 40 years may be explained by what?

A. Increase in the number of breech births.

B. Rh incompatibility.

C. Increased medical control of childbirth.

D. Rise in sexually transmitted diseases.

Your answer:

18. A loud noise causes 8-week-old Simeon to extend his arms outwards and extend his legs and head. Which reflex does this illustrate?

A. Babinksi.

B. Moro.

C. Palmar.

D. Rooting.

Your answer:

19. Vision is less well developed at birth for what reason?

A. Optic nerves are not fully myelinated and interconnectivity between neurons is limited.

B. Visual acuity is restricted and axons are not fully myelinated.

C. The optic nerves are not fully formed or myelinated.

D. Neurons of the visual cortex are not yet formed.

Your answer:

20. Behaviours that are not that susceptible to environmental influence are said to be what?

A. Canalised.

B. Innate.

C. Passive.

D. Plastic.

Your answer: ☐

Extended multiple-choice question

Maternal age is just one of the most common threats to typical prenatal development, also known as teratogens. Risks to the child and parent are greater for mothers aged 30 or above; however, children born to teenage mothers are also at risk of, for example, premature birth and higher rates of infant mortality. Additional factors may also play a part in typical prenatal development.

Below is a list of potential confounding factors that may pose risks to prenatal development. Select five factors that are *most likely* to present a risk to typical development of children born to teenage mothers.

A. Low income

B. High alcohol exposure

C. Drug use

D. Poor education

E. Sexually transmitted diseases

F. Exposure to environmental teratogens, e.g. lead, x-rays, etc.

G. Living in a deprived area

H. High stress levels

I. Lack of support from family members

J. Limited access to good prenatal care

K. Malnourishment

L. Disease, e.g. mumps, measles, rubella, etc.

Essay questions for Chapter 2

Once you have completed the MCQs above you are ready to tackle some essay questions. You might like to select three or four topics and make notes on them. One way of doing this is to create a concept map. The first question has been done for you and you can see how the knowledge required links to some of the MCQs in this chapter.

1. Critically evaluate the impact of both environmental and maternal factors on typical prenatal development.

2. Discuss how teratogens illustrate the relative importance of both nature and nurture on typical prenatal development.

3. Evaluate the extent to which the embryonic period is the most critical for typical prenatal development.

4. Critically reflect upon the idea that women over the age of 40 are at greater risk of experiencing complications during pregnancy and childbirth than younger women.

5. Critically evaluate the effectiveness of prenatal learning programmes on long-term cognitive development.

6. Critically discuss how both social and cultural factors may account for the increase in the number of Caesarean births in recent years.

7. With reference to research and theory, discuss how the use of methods of pain relief during childbirth may affect the relationship between the mother and newborn.

8. To what extent are the neonate's abilities determined by heredity or the environment?

Chapter 2 essay question 1: concept map

Critically evaluate the impact of both environmental and maternal factors on typical development.

The concept map below provides an example of the topic areas that you might include when writing your essay. Remember that it is important to link your answers to other topic areas not covered in this chapter. This question requires you to consider both environmental and maternal factors on typical development. Good answers to this question will draw upon issues discussed in Chapter 1 of this book, specifically the nature–nurture debate and theories of human development.

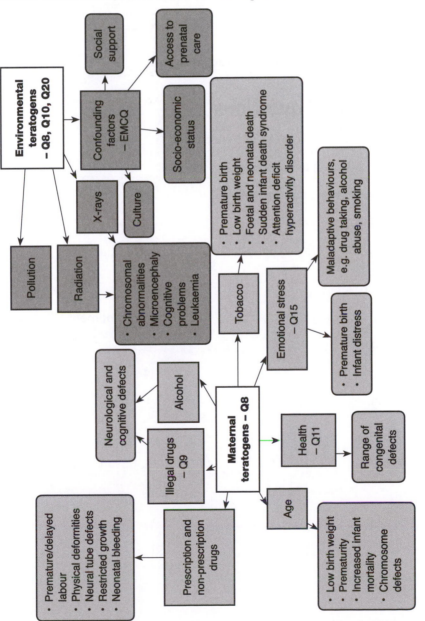

Chapter 3
Motor and perceptual development

This chapter provides questions relating to the sequence of motor development, the development of gross and fine motor skills, the development of the senses and intermodal perception.

Select one of the possible answers for each question.

Foundation level questions

1. Gross motor development refers to which skills?

    A. Crawling, standing and walking.

    B. Reaching, grasping and sitting.

    C. Crawling, reaching and walking.

    D. Building a tower, playing pat-a-cake and walking on tiptoe.

    Your answer: ☐

2. Which of the following is an example of fine motor development?

    A. Crawling.

    B. Skipping.

    C. Grasping.

    D. Standing.

    Your answer: ☐

3. Gross and fine motor development typically occurs at what age?

   A. 2 years.

   B. 3 years.

   C. 4 years.

   D. 5 years.

Your answer: ☐

4. A child can usually hold their head upright at what age?

   A. 2 months old.

   B. 6 weeks old.

   C. 2 weeks old.

   D. 3 months old.

Your answer: ☐

5. What is proprioception?

   A. The effect of external influences on movement such as reflexes.

   B. Visual guidance of the arms and legs.

   C. The child's ability to reach towards an object in front of them.

   D. The sensation of movement and location arising from bodily stimulations.

Your answer: ☐

6. The ability of a newborn infant to swipe an object placed in front of them is known as what?

   A. Prereaching.

   B. Directed reaching.

   C. Proprioception.

   D. Ulnar grasp.

Your answer: ☐

7. The opposable use of the thumb and index finger in a well-coordinated manner is referred to as what?

   A. Ulnar grasp.

   B. Palmar grasp.

   C. Pincer grasp.

   D. Babinski reflex.

   Your answer: ☐

8. Gesell and McGraw (1935) suggested that motor development occurred as a result of what?

   A. Conditioned reflexes.

   B. Maturation.

   C. Experience.

   D. Increasing cognitive ability.

   Your answer: ☐

9. Contemporary research on motor development emphasises the role of what?

   A. Environmental transactions.

   B. Cultural influences.

   C. Environmental and cultural influences.

   D. Individual differences.

   Your answer: ☐

10. The process of acquiring increasingly complex systems of action is known as what?

   A. Ecological systems theory.

   B. Intermodal perception.

   C. Dynamic systems theory.

   D. Maturation.

   Your answer: ☐

11. Thelen and Smith (1998) proposed that each new motor skill is the product of how many factors?

    A. 2.

    B. 3.

    C. 4.

    D. 5.

Your answer: ☐

12. Which of the following factors is not part of dynamic systems theory?

    A. Central nervous system development.

    B. Intellectual capacities of the child.

    C. The goal of the child.

    D. Environmental supports for the child.

Your answer: ☐

13. Sitting, crawling and walking are not typically encouraged in which cultures?

    A. Japanese.

    B. Western.

    C. Rural Indian.

    D. Both A and C.

Your answer: ☐

Advanced level questions

14. Panna is now able to steer and pedal her tricycle. How old is Panna?

    A. 2 years old.

    B. 3–4 years old.

    C. 5–6 years old.

    D. 7 years old.

Your answer: ☐

15. At the end of early childhood children are typically able to do what?

    A. Construct puzzles, use a knife and fork and clothe themselves.

    B. Skip, throw and catch.

    C. Fasten their shoes, hop, climb a climbing frame.

    D. All of the above.

Your answer: ☐

16. Golomb (2004) suggests that drawing ability is influenced by what?

    A. Improved planning and spatial understanding.

    B. Maturationally determined factors.

    C. Interaction between maturation and experience.

    D. Cognitive, perceptual and maturational factors.

Your answer: ☐

17. Newborn children prefer to look at patterned rather than plain stimuli. As children get older they show a preference for what?

    A. Larger patterns.

    B. Less complexity.

    C. Greater complexity.

    D. Brighter patterns.

Your answer: ☐

18. Zoe can now discriminate between blue blocks and red ones. What skill has Zoe developed?

    A. Depth perception.

    B. Visual acuity.

    C. Visual cliff.

    D. Colour perception.

Your answer: ☐

19. The rapid development of intermodal perception has been attributed to what?

   A. Exposure to environmental cues.

   B. Improvements in contrast sensitivity.

   C. Biological priming.

   D. Kinetic depth cues.

Your answer: ☐

20. According to Gibson and Gibson (1970) which of the following is an ability generally shown by infants?

   A. They actively search for invariant features of the environment.

   B. They are impressive perceivers of amodal properties.

   C. They are statistical analysers of sound patterns.

   D. They perceive depth cues in a fixed order.

Your answer: ☐

21. Differentiation theory highlights the importance of what?

   A. Recognition.

   B. Analysis.

   C. Exposure.

   D. Priming.

Your answer: ☐

22. Which of the following visual abilities is not developed in 6–8 month old infants?

   A. Visual acuity of about 20/100.

   B. Detection of subjective boundaries in patterns.

   C. The ability to track objects with smooth eye movements.

   D. Detection of objects represented by incomplete drawings.

Your answer: ☐

23. Which of the following visual abilities is not developed in infants younger than one month old?

  A. The ability to respond to kinetic cues.

  B. Face perception.

  C. Sensitivity to binocular cues.

  D. Pattern recognition.

Your answer: ☐

24. Infants' preference for Mozart minuets with pauses between phrases to those with awkward breaks illustrates what?

  A. Musical phrasing.

  B. Kinetic responsiveness.

  C. Sensitivity to stereopsis.

  D. Recognition of complex patterns.

Your answer: ☐

25. Neonates cannot focus their eyes well for what reason?

  A. Because the optic nerve is not fully developed.

  B. Because they lack cognitive ability to make sense of visual cues.

  C. Because they have not been exposed to sufficient visual stimulation.

  D. Because they lack visual acuity.

Your answer: ☐

26. What do researchers believe about the relationship between motor and perceptual development?

  A. Motor development occurs first and facilitates perceptual development.

  B. They are dependent upon each other.

  C. Perceptual development occurs first and facilitates motor development.

  D. They develop independently.

Your answer: ☐

Extended multiple-choice question

Researchers have identified that gross and fine motor skills develop in a certain sequence. Below is a list of selected milestones in gross and fine motor development that should typically occur in the first two years of life. Complete the table by placing the motor skills in the correct order at which they develop.

Motor skill	Average age achieved
	6 weeks
	2 months
	3 months
	7 months
	9 months
	11 months
	12 months
	14 months
	23 months
	25 months

A. Grasps a block

B. Holds head upright

C. Jumps in place

D. Plays pat-a-cake

E. Rolls from side to back

F. Scribbles

G. Sits without support

H. Stands without support

I. Walks on tiptoe

J. Walks without support

Essay questions for Chapter 3

Once you have completed the MCQs above you are ready to tackle some essay questions. You might like to select three or four topics and make notes on them. One way of doing this is to create a concept map. The first question has been done for you and you can see how the knowledge required links to some of the MCQs in this chapter.

1. Discuss the role of perception in the development of motor skills in infancy.

2. Critically evaluate the role of maturation versus experience on the development of motor skills in infancy.

3. Discuss the extent to which dynamic systems theory provides an adequate explanation of motor development.

4. Describe and evaluate how changes in motor and perceptual development in childhood influence a child's ability to draw.

5. With reference to research evidence, discuss how intermodal perception can foster all aspects of psychological development.

6. Discuss the role of Gibson's differentiation theory in the development of motor skills.

7. Discuss how motor development is shaped by biological, psychological and environmental factors.

8. Discuss the claim that perceptual development occurs only during infancy.

Chapter 3 essay question 1: concept map

Discuss the role of perception in the development of motor skills in infancy.

The concept map below provides an example of the topic areas that you might include when writing your essay. Remember that it is important to link your answers to other topic areas not covered in this chapter. This question requires you to evaluate the relationship of perception and motor skill development. Good answers to this question will acknowledge the bi-directional relationship between these factors but also consider the role of the wider cultural context of development and its impact on the development of motor skills.

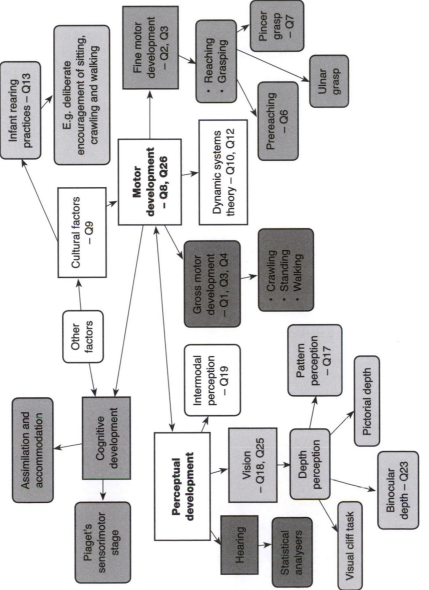

Chapter 4
Attachment

This chapter provides questions relating to theories of attachment, attachment security, cultural variations in attachment, factors affecting attachment, multiple attachments and the impact of attachment on later development.

Select one of the possible answers for each question.

Foundation level questions

1. Psychoanalytic theories describe attachment as what?

    A. A learned instinct.

    B. A product of reinforced behaviours.

    C. Satisfaction of needs, for example feeding by the mother.

    D. An innate set of behaviours.

    Your answer:

2. Behaviourist theories view attachment as what?

    A. A product of reinforced behaviours.

    B. A learned instinct.

    C. An innate set of behaviours.

    D. Satisfaction of needs, for example feeding by the mother.

    Your answer:

3. Bowlby's ethological theory of attachment was influenced by which branch of psychology?

    A. Evolutionary psychology.

    B. Biological psychology.

    C. Cognitive psychology.

    D. Social psychology.

    Your answer:

4. According to Bowlby attachment typically develops over how many phases?

   A. 3.

   B. 4.

   C. 6.

   D. Attachment is viewed as a continuous process.

Your answer: ☐

5. In which of the following situations is it most likely that separation anxiety will occur?

   A. When the child's primary caregiver leaves.

   B. When the adult does not respond to the child's demands.

   C. When the adult is away from their child for an extended period of time.

   D. When a stranger offers comfort to a child in emotional distress.

Your answer: ☐

6. Expectations about the availability of attachment figures and likelihood of providing support during stressful times are known as what?

   A. The Strange Situation.

   B. Attachment security.

   C. Goodness of fit model.

   D. An internal working model.

Your answer: ☐

7. The Strange Situation is a laboratory procedure developed by whom?

   A. John Bowlby.

   B. Sigmund Freud.

   C. Mary Ainsworth.

   D. Harry Harlow.

Your answer: ☐

8. The Strange Situation takes the baby through how many short episodes in which brief separations and reunions from the parent occur?

    A. 7.

    B. 8.

    C. 4.

    D. 3.

Your answer: ☐

9. Which of the following is not an episode in the Strange Situation?

    A. Parent is seated while the baby plays with toys.

    B. Parent leaves the room. Stranger responds to the baby and offers comfort if the baby is upset.

    C. Researcher introduces both the parent and the baby to the stranger.

    D. Parent returns and offers comfort if necessary. Stranger leaves the room.

Your answer: ☐

10. A major criticism of early research examining the stability of attachment is what?

    A. Failure to account for stressful life events.

    B. Research mainly focused on middle-class families.

    C. Failure to account for cultural differences.

    D. Both B and C.

Your answer: ☐

11. A child may develop _____ if the quality of caregiving improves or if he or she forms a bond with an individual outside of the immediate family.

    A. Resilience.

    B. Compliance.

    C. Empathy.

    D. Vulnerability.

Your answer: ☐

12. Which researchers developed the first measure of adult attachment?

    A. Ainsworth and Bowlby.

    B. Hazan and Shaver.

    C. Bartholomew and Horowitz.

    D. Brennan and Clark.

Your answer: ☐

13. Which of the following is not a measure of adult attachment?

    A. Relationship Questionnaire (RQ-CV).

    B. Experiences in Close Relationships (ECR).

    C. Adult Attachment Inventory – Revised (AAI-R).

    D. Experiences in Close Relationships – Revised (ECR-R).

Your answer: ☐

Advanced level questions

14. Two-year-old Grace asks her parents to read her a story before they leave her with a babysitter. Grace's parents tell her that they'll be back later after she has gone to sleep. According to Bowlby, Grace is in which phase of attachment?

    A. Pre-attachment phase.

    B. Attachment in the making phase.

    C. Clear-cut attachment phase.

    D. Formation of a reciprocal relationship phase.

Your answer: ☐

15. The clear-cut attachment phase is characterised by:

    A. Display of separation anxiety.

    B. Grasping, smiling and gazing towards the caregiver.

    C. Negotiation with the caregiver to alter goals.

    D. Differing responses to a familiar caregiver than a stranger.

Your answer: ☐

16. Femi was born in the United States and Daniel was born in Germany. In contrast to Femi, Daniel is more likely to show more _____ attachment than Femi.

A. Secure.

B. Avoidant.

C. Resistant.

D. Disorientated.

Your answer:

17. It's Katie's first day at school and as she says goodbye to her mum, she becomes very upset. Katie's teacher manages to calm Katie down by assuring her that her mum will be back at the end of the day. When Katie's mum picks her up from school, she runs up and hugs her. Which form of attachment was Katie displaying?

A. Disorientated attachment.

B. Resistant attachment.

C. Avoidant attachment.

D. Secure attachment.

Your answer:

18. Bogital, a young boy in a Bulgarian orphanage, displayed excessive over-friendliness to unfamiliar adults, in addition to other emotional and social problems. Staff turnover was so high that he had had over 30 caregivers by the age of 5. Which of the following is most likely to account for his excessive friendliness?

A. Limited opportunity for attachment.

B. Insensitive caregiving.

C. Emotionally reactive temperament.

D. Separation anxiety.

Your answer:

19. When 5-year-old Harry is upset he runs to his _____ for comfort. When he wants to play he seeks the company of his _____.

   A. Father, mother.

   B. Mother, mother.

   C. Mother, father.

   D. Father, father.

Your answer: ☐

20. Positive sibling interaction and pre-schoolers' support of a distressed younger sibling has been explained by what?

   A. Maternal harshness and lack of involvement.

   B. Maternal warmth towards all siblings.

   C. Child temperament.

   D. Frequent play between parent and child.

Your answer: ☐

21. Rosemary and her husband both have full-time, demanding jobs and decide to put their 1-year-old twins into full-time childcare. What impact may their decision have on their children's later adjustment?

   A. More likely to develop insecure attachment.

   B. No negative effect if the children are provided with high-quality childcare for only a limited period of time.

   C. More likely to develop emotional and behavioural problems.

   D. Both A and B.

Your answer: ☐

22. Jane is asked to recall her childhood memories of attachment experiences. This technique is used to assess what?

   A. Parents' internal working models.

   B. Quality of caregiving.

   C. Number of enduring relationships.

   D. Potential psychological problems in later development.

Your answer: ☐

23. Research has shown that negative life events can weaken the link between an individual's attachment security in infancy and a secure internal working model in adulthood. What does this suggest about the nature of development?

A. Development is plastic and multidimensional.

B. Development is a discontinuous process.

C. Development is unidirectional.

D. Development is only affected by environmental influences.

Your answer: ☐

24. According to Brennan, Clark and Shaver (1998), an individual who displays a dismissive attachment style is likely to score what?

A. High attachment-related avoidance and low attachment-related anxiety.

B. Low attachment-related avoidance and high attachment-related anxiety.

C. High attachment-related avoidance and high attachment-related anxiety.

D. Low attachment-related avoidance and low attachment-related anxiety.

Your answer: ☐

25. Monira comments: 'I am uncomfortable being without close relationships, but I sometimes worry that others don't value me as much as I value them.' According to Bartholomew and Horowitz which style of attachment is Monira describing?

A. Secure.

B. Dismissive.

C. Preoccupied.

D. Fearful.

Your answer: ☐

26. According to Hazan and Shaver's (1987) three-category measure of adult attachment, which of the following is not an example of anxious-resistant attachment?

   A. I find that others are reluctant to get as close as I would like.

   B. I often worry that my partner doesn't really love me or won't want to stay with me.

   C. I want to get very close to my partner and this sometimes scares people away.

   D. I am somewhat uncomfortable being close to others.

Your answer: ☐

Extended multiple-choice question

Complete the following paragraph using the items listed overleaf. Not all of the items will be needed and each item can only be used once.

Attachment theorists including _____ have suggested that the quality of an infant's attachment to their caregiver has salient consequences for later development. Infants who establish _____ should develop into confident children who are able to form good relationships with their peers. For example, _____ found that securely attached children were more enthusiastic, frustrated less easily and were more persistent in finding a solution to a problem-solving task than _____ attached infants when observed at 18 and 24 months of age. This suggests that early _____ have a profound effect on later social, emotional and cognitive development. However, longitudinal research has found that this is not always the case. Consequently, _____ of caregiving has been identified as a factor that may determine whether _____ is maintained in later development. Initial security of attachment in infancy provides a good starting point for a positive parent–child relationship; however, this is _____ upon the quality of the child's future relationships. This indicates that attachment is not always _____ over time and highlights the _____ relationship between parent and child in the development of attachment.

Optional items

A. attachment security

B. Bowlby

C. bi-directional

D. continuity

E. conditional

F. Freud

G. important

H. insecurely

I. learned behaviours

J. Matas et al. (1978)

K. multiple attachments

L. quality

M. secure attachments

N. social experiences

O. stable

Essay questions for Chapter 4

Once you have completed the MCQs above you are ready to tackle some essay questions. You might like to select three or four topics and make notes on them. One way of doing this is to create a concept map. The first question has been done for you and you can see how the knowledge required links to some of the MCQs in this chapter.

1. Analyse the extent to which Bowlby's ethological theory provides an adequate explanation of attachment.

2. Critically evaluate the idea that infants are predisposed to form an attachment with a single person.

3. To what extent can the 'Strange Situation' developed by Ainsworth be used to assess the quality of attachment?

4. Explain the relative influence of both children's and adults' behaviours upon the formation of attachment.

5. Discuss the extent to which the quality of caregiving can solely explain attachment security.

6. With reference to research and theory, discuss why there may be cultural variation in attachment patterns.

7. Reflect upon the extent to which Ainsworth's four types of attachment are only relevant to development in infancy.

8. Critically evaluate the claim that failure to establish a secure attachment during the first few months of life will result in difficulties in later emotional development.

9. Discuss the extent to which attachment patterns observed among adults are similar to those observed among children.

Chapter 4 essay question 1: concept map

Analyse the extent to which Bowlby's ethological theory provides an adequate explanation of attachment.

The concept map below provides an example of the topic areas that you might include when writing your essay. Remember that it is important to link your answers to other topic areas not covered in this chapter. This question requires you to critically evaluate Bowlby's theory of attachment formation. Good answers to this question will consider not only the innate factors associated with attachment but also cultural and environmental influences. It is also important that you make links to other attachment theories and consider methodological issues surrounding the measurement of attachment.

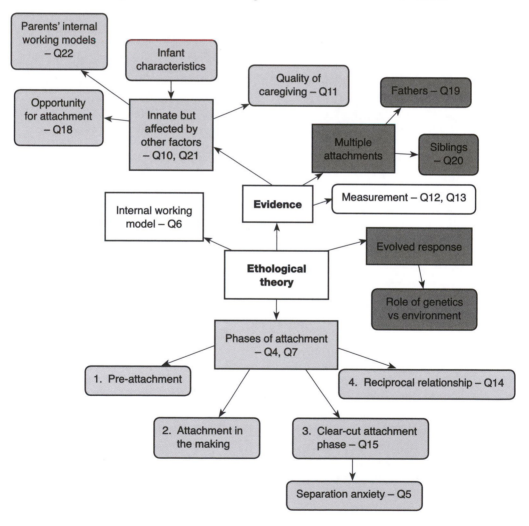

Chapter 5
Language development

This chapter provides questions relating to theories of language development, preverbal communication, semantic development, syntax development and the development of pragmatics.

Select one of the possible answers for each question.

Foundation level questions

1. Children typically speak their first words at approximately _____ months of age.

    A. 6.

    B. 12.

    C. 18.

    D. 24

    Your answer:

2. At what age do babies begin to babble?

    A. 3 months.

    B. 6 months.

    C. 9 months.

    D. 12 months.

    Your answer: [ ]

3. The study of phonology refers to what?

    A. Meaningful sounds.

    B. Word meanings.

    C. Grammatical rules.

    D. Spelling ability.

    Your answer: [ ]

4. The way in which we develop knowledge of word meanings and vocabulary is known as what?

A. Semantics.

B. Phonology.

C. Pragmatics.

D. Syntax.

Your answer: ☐

5. According to the behaviourist perspective, children's speech develops through what?

A. Observational learning.

B. Social support.

C. Operant conditioning.

D. Maturation.

Your answer: ☐

6. Which of the following do behaviourists believe is not involved in language development?

A. Imitation.

B. Classical conditioning.

C. Operant conditioning.

D. Innate mental structures.

Your answer: ☐

7. According to Chomsky, language is the product of what?

A. Positive parental feedback of sounds and utterances.

B. Unlearned, innate mental structures.

C. Imitation of what others say, resulting in learning of utterances.

D. Scaffolding and social support.

Your answer: ☐

8. Which of the following does interactionist theory emphasise?

   A. Language development should be viewed in relation to social development.

   B. Language development is an interplay between environmental and biological factors.

   C. Language development requires scaffolding by the parent.

   D. All of the above.

Your answer: ☐

9. Using pointing gestures to bring an object to another's attention is known as what?

   A. Protodeclarative pointing.

   B. Protoimperative pointing.

   C. Semantic development.

   D. Pseudo dialogue.

Your answer: ☐

10. The process through which children attend to the same object, person or event as another person is known as _____ attention.

   A. Sustained.

   B. Selective.

   C. Joint.

   D. Flexible.

Your answer: ☐

11. Sounds which make up a specific language are called what?

   A. Pragmatics.

   B. Syntax.

   C. Semantics.

   D. Phonemes.

Your answer: ☐

12. Which three constraints on word meaning were proposed by Markman (1989)?

    A. Whole-object, overextension, underextension.

    B. Syntactic bootstrapping, overextension, underextension.

    C. Whole-object, taxonomic, mutual exclusivity.

    D. Taxonomic, mutual exclusivity, syntactic bootstrapping.

Your answer: ☐

Advanced level questions

13. Isabel points to a picture of a cow and says 'doggie'. This is an example of what?

    A. Overextension.

    B. Underextension.

    C. Whole-object constraint.

    D. Violation of mutual exclusivity.

Your answer: ☐

14. The presence of errors in semantic development suggests what?

    A. Children use syntactic information to figure out the meaning of words.

    B. Word learning is an active process in which children construct hypotheses about objects and labels.

    C. Social support is necessary for word learning.

    D. Children use constraints to determine the meaning of words.

Your answer: ☐

15. Jake is eight years old. By the time he reaches adolescence his vocabulary will reach approximately how many words?

    A. 20,000 words.

    B. 30,000 words.

    C. 40,000 words.

    D. 60,000 words.

Your answer: ☐

16. Which of the following is an example of telegraphic speech?

   A. Big dogs.

   B. I can read.

   C. Take off my shoes.

   D. Give juice.

Your answer: ☐

17. Esther is 3 years old and can now add grammatical morphemes. Which of the following sentences is she likely to say?

   A. I won't do it.

   B. He dance.

   C. There dogs.

   D. Daddy read.

Your answer: ☐

18. Gurdeep is 5 years old. He is able to adjust the level of his speech depending upon who he is talking to. This is known as what?

   A. Egocentric speech.

   B. A turnabout.

   C. A speech register.

   D. Speech act theory.

Your answer: ☐

19. Daniel comments to his friend Ben, 'Well, aren't you a little ray of sunshine today.' This is an example of what?

   A. Conversational implicature.

   B. Say–mean distinction.

   C. A cooperative principle.

   D. Locutionary act.

Your answer: ☐

20. A young child may often miscommunicate information to their listener due to a lack of what?

A. Sociolinguistic knowledge.

B. Syntactic development.

C. Referential communication skills.

D. Illocutionary force.

Your answer:

21. Sarah's mum comments, 'Your room is a tip.' Sarah understands this to mean, 'Tidy your room.' This is an example of what?

A. An illocutionary force.

B. Conversational implicature.

C. Shading.

D. Pragmatics.

Your answer:

22. The _____ principle states that participants in a communicative exchange are expected to make contributions to a conversation in accordance with the purpose or direction of the exchange.

A. Conversational.

B. Cooperative.

C. Speech act.

D. Perlocutionary.

Your answer:

23. Your housemate returns from their first day in their new job. You ask, 'How was your day?' Your friend replies, 'It's raining outside ...' Which one of Grice's maxims have they violated?

   A. Quantity.

   B. Quality.

   C. Manner.

   D. Relation.

Your answer: ▢

24. Elena is proofreading her friend's essay and comments that some of her sentences are not grammatically correct. Elena has acquired what?

   A. Metalinguistic awareness.

   B. Referential communication skills.

   C. Semantic bootstrapping.

   D. Communicative intent.

Your answer: ▢

Extended multiple-choice question

Complete the following paragraph using the items listed overleaf. Not all of the items will be needed and each item can only be used once.

_____ is the ability to learn _____ languages at a time. Children can become bilingual by either acquiring both languages at the same time during _____ childhood or learning a second language after the first. Learning a second language in childhood is often _____ than learning later in life. This is because a _____ period exists for language mastery. The ability to learn an additional language is thought to decrease in a _____ and _____ way from childhood to adulthood but no specific age for decline in language learning ability has been identified. Research evidence has suggested that bilingual children often do better on tests of _____ and _____. They may also have a greater awareness of grammatical errors, or _____.

Optional items

A. age-related

B. bilingualism

C. cognitive flexibility

D. continuous

E. critical

F. discontinuous

G. early

H. easier

I. more difficult

J. metalinguistic awareness

K. middle

L. normative

M. referential communication skills

N. sensitive

O. selective attention

P. two

Essay questions for Chapter 5

Once you have completed the MCQs above you are ready to tackle some essay questions. You might like to select three or four topics and make notes on them. One way of doing this is to create a concept map. The first question has been done for you and you can see how the knowledge required links to some of the MCQs in this chapter.

1. Critically evaluate two theories of language development with reference to their stance on innate versus environmental influences.

2. Discuss why the interactionist perspective is regarded as the most attractive view of language acquisition.

3. Discuss how a primary school teacher might foster syntactic development in their pupils.

4. Discuss the extent to which language development is a continuous process.

5. To what extent is children's use of grammar a function of their cognitive abilities?

6. Discuss how the development of pragmatics can explain problems in children's speech production.

7. Critically evaluate the claim that bilingualism can enhance reading development.

8. Discuss the evidence that claims that learning a second language promotes metalinguistic awareness.

Chapter 5 essay question 1: concept map

Critically evaluate two theories of language development with reference to their stance on innate versus environmental influences.

The concept map below provides an example of the topic areas that you might include when writing your essay. Remember that it is important to link your answers to other topic areas not covered in this chapter. This question requires you to describe and evaluate two main theories of language development. Good answers to this question will not only consider the strengths and weaknesses of these theories but also consider the relative influence of nature and nurture discussed in Chapter 1 of this book.

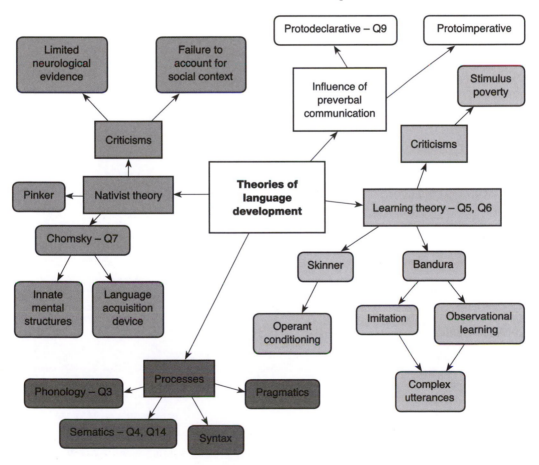

Chapter 6
Play and peer interaction

This chapter provides questions relating to theories of play, the development of play in childhood, gender differences in play, the impact of play on cognitive and social development, peer acceptance and friendship.

Select one of the possible answers for each question.

Foundation level questions

1. Early observational studies of children's play were conducted by who?

  A. Piaget.

  B. Parten.

  C. Vygotsky.

  D. Freud.

Your answer: ☐

2. Which of the following is not a type of play identified by Parten?

  A. Cooperative.

  B. Associative.

  C. Parallel.

  D. Make-believe.

Your answer: ☐

3. What is traditionally viewed as the most common form of play among 4-year-old children?

  A. Cooperative.

  B. Associative.

  C. Parallel.

  D. Onlooker.

Your answer: ☐

4. When does parallel play occur?

   A. When children play beside rather than with other children.

   B. When children play by themselves in a way which is different to those around them.

   C. When a child watches others play but does not join in.

   D. When children play games together.

Your answer: ☐

5. In contrast to Parten's focus on social interaction, Piaget emphasised what?

   A. Cognitive complexity of play.

   B. Cultural aspects of play.

   C. Play as therapy.

   D. Play as a means of exercising skills.

Your answer: ☐

6. According to Piaget, make-believe play develops over how many phases?

   A. 2.

   B. 3.

   C. 4.

   D. 5.

Your answer: ☐

7. Make-believe play has been associated with what?

   A. Attention, memory and literacy.

   B. Perspective taking, creativity and imagination.

   C. Academic attainment, temperament and empathy.

   D. Both A and B.

Your answer: ☐

8. Sex differences in sporting ability may be accounted for by what?

   A. Muscle mass.

   B. Genetics and parental beliefs about the value of sport.

   C. Parental beliefs about the value of sport.

   D. Height.

Your answer: ☐

9. Which of the following occurs during middle childhood?

   A. Games such as 'tag' become more common.

   B. There is an increase in make-believe play.

   C. Children often invent their own games.

   D. Both A and C.

Your answer: ☐

10. A clique may be defined as what?

   A. A close-knit group of friends held together by common interests and values.

   B. A group of individuals organised on the basis of reputation and stereotypes.

   C. A group of individuals organised in terms of dominance, e.g. assertiveness.

   D. A close-knit group of friends based on status.

Your answer: ☐

Advanced level questions

11. Two children are acting out a scene from their favourite film. What type of play are the children engaging in?

   A. Parallel play.

   B. Constructive play.

   C. Make-believe play.

   D. Associative play.

Your answer: ☐

12. Seven-year-old Dinesh spends a lot of his time engaging in sociodramatic play. Which of the following would most closely describe Dinesh?

   A. More egocentric.

   B. An artistic child.

   C. Cognitively advanced.

   D. Unable to make friends easily.

Your answer: ☐

13. Dominance hierarchies typically emerge during which developmental phase?

   A. Infancy.

   B. Early childhood.

   C. Middle-to-late childhood.

   D. Adolescence.

Your answer: ☐

14. In middle-to-late childhood, what is the developmental trend in peer interaction?

   A. Increasing contact with peers, for example more diverse peer group, and less supervision.

   B. Increased time spent with peers centring on intimacy and self-disclosure.

   C. Greater understanding of perspective taking enhances theory of mind.

   D. The emergence of dominance hierarchies.

Your answer: ☐

15. Parents who provide frequent informal peer play are an example of what?

   A. Direct parental influence.

   B. Indirect parental influence.

   C. Both direct and indirect parental influence.

   D. Responsive parenting.

Your answer: ☐

16. Low peer status may result in what?

    A. Academic difficulties such as learned helplessness.

    B. Increased feelings of loneliness.

    C. Truancy.

    D. All of the above.

Your answer:

17. Sociometric nominations are used to measure what?

    A. Dominance hierarchies.

    B. Friendship formation.

    C. Theory of mind.

    D. Peer status.

Your answer:

18. Joe displays high levels of conflict, hostility towards others and impulsive behaviour. Which sociometric category would Joe fit into?

    A. Aggressive rejected.

    B. Non-aggressive rejected.

    C. Controversial.

    D. Neglected.

Your answer:

19. Ndidi is 14 years old. When asked about the meaning of friendship, which characteristics is she most likely to suggest are important?

    A. Similar interests and intimacy.

    B. Trust and similar interests.

    C. Loyalty and intimacy.

    D. Sensitivity and acceptance.

Your answer: ☐

20. Which of the following statements about peer relationships in adolescence is false?

   A. The formation of cliques and crowds is linked to parenting practices.

   B. The self-concept is a mediating factor in the formation of cliques and crowds.

   C. Cliques are only ever made up of same-sex members.

   D. Close friendship can improve attitude towards and involvement in school.

Your answer: ☐

Extended multiple-choice question

Complete the following paragraph using the items listed overleaf. Not all of the items will be needed and each item can only be used once.

Friendship can be defined as a relationship between two or more individuals that requires commitment and _____. _____ tape-recorded conversations of children and identified _____ processes involved in friendship formation that distinguished play patterns of children with their best friends compared to with strangers. He also suggested that the focus of friendship is thought to change with age. In early childhood, the goal of peer interaction is to achieve _____ whereas older children are more concerned with _____ and _____. In adolescence the focus of friendship is much more on _____. Sullivan (1953) suggested that friendship serves a number of functions, for example, to provide affection and promote the growth of _____. Rubin and Coplan (1992) suggest additional functions of friendship including providing a context for transmitting _____. Friendships have also been argued to offer a _____ outside of the family setting.

Optional items

A. coordinated play

B. friendship quality

C. four

D. Gottman (1983)

E. identity

F. interpersonal sensitivity

G. liking

H. peer acceptance

I. reciprocity

J. rejection

K. secure base

L. self-disclosure

M. self-esteem

N. six

O. social norms

Essay questions for Chapter 6

Once you have completed the MCQs above you are ready to tackle some essay questions. You might like to select three or four topics and make notes on them. One way of doing this is to create a concept map. The first question has been done for you and you can see how the knowledge required links to some of the MCQs in this chapter.

1. Discuss the importance of play for social development.

2. Describe and evaluate how make-believe play can enhance cognitive development.

3. Evaluate the importance of play for early social interaction.

4. Discuss the impact of parental influence on the development of early peer relations.

5. Critically evaluate the role of motor development on play during middle childhood.

6. Discuss how peer interaction differs between early and middle childhood.

7. Evaluate the role of sex differences in play during middle childhood.

8. Describe and evaluate the impact of low peer status on emotional development during childhood.

Chapter 6 essay question 1: concept map

Discuss the importance of play for social development.

The concept map below provides an example of the topic areas that you might include when writing your essay. Remember that it is important to link your answers to other topic areas not covered in this chapter. This question requires you to describe and evaluate the role of play and peer interaction on social development. Good answers to this question will consider the various theories of the development of play and also draw upon issues discussed in Chapter 8 of this book, development of prosocial behaviour. It is also important that you consider the importance of peer interaction across childhood and adolescence and do not focus solely on early childhood.

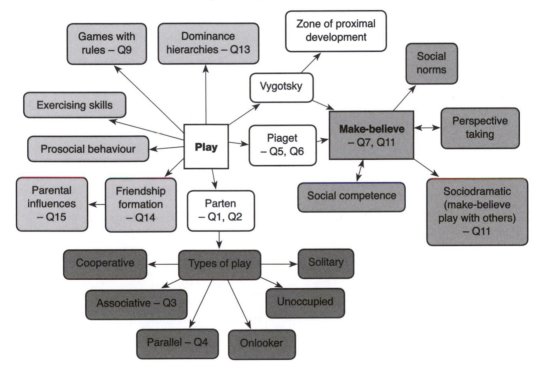

Chapter 7
Cognitive development

This chapter provides questions relating to Piaget's theory of cognitive development, Vygotsky's perspective of cognitive development and information processing theory.

Select one of the possible answers for each question.

Foundation level questions

1. Piaget's theory of cognitive development was influenced by what?

    A. Behaviourism.

    B. Psychoanalysis.

    C. Biology.

    D. Functionalism.

    Your answer:

2. Which of the following displays Piaget's stages of cognitive development in the correct sequence?

    A. Sensorimotor, preoperational, concrete operational, formal operational.

    B. Preoperational, operational, post operational.

    C. Premotor, sensory operational, operational, abstract thought.

    D. Sensory, concrete operational, formal operational.

    Your answer:

3. What term did Piaget give to the interrelated set of cognitive structures?

    A. Processes.

    B. Schemes.

    C. Stages.

    D. Outputs.

    Your answer:

4. Which term is used to refer to the process in which a child interprets the world through currently available schemes?

   A. Accommodation.

   B. Adaptation.

   C. Equilibrium.

   D. Assimilation.

Your answer: ☐

5. Which term is used to refer to revising schemes to incorporate newly acquired information from the environment?

   A. Adaptation.

   B. Accommodation.

   C. Equilibrium.

   D. Assimilation.

Your answer: ☐

6. Primary circular reactions typically occur in which developmental stage?

   A. Sensorimotor.

   B. Preoperational.

   C. Formal operational.

   D. Concrete operational.

Your answer: ☐

7. Egocentrism refers to what?

   A. Children's tendency to see things only from their own point of view.

   B. The tendency for children to attribute lifelike qualities to inanimate objects.

   C. Children's ability to focus only on one thing at a time.

   D. A child's belief that the world revolves around themselves.

Your answer: ☐

8. Object permanence refers to what?

A. The ability of objects to stay in the same place.

B. The idea that objects continue to exist despite the fact we cannot perceive them.

C. A child's ability to think using representations as opposed to actions.

D. Both B and C.

Your answer: ☐

9. How old are children in the concrete operational stage, according to Piaget?

A. 0–2.

B. 2–7.

C. 7–11.

D. 11+.

Your answer: ☐

10. Hypothetico-deductive reasoning is thought to develop at what age?

A. 0–2.

B. 2–7.

C. 7–11.

D. 11+.

Your answer: ☐

11. The ability to evaluate the validity of verbal statements without concrete examples is known as what?

A. Hypothetico-deductive reasoning.

B. Propositional thinking.

C. Transitive inference.

D. Conservation.

Your answer: ☐

12. Formal operational thinking is typically what?

   A. Logical.

   B. Abstract.

   C. Egocentric.

   D. Emotional.

Your answer: ☐

13. According to the information processing approach, the sensory register refers to which of the following?

   A. The permanent unlimited knowledge base.

   B. The part of the working memory that coordinates the flow of information.

   C. The aspect of memory where sights and sounds are stored briefly.

   D. The aspect of the mind that facilitates memory and problem-solving.

Your answer: ☐

14. An organised set of mental states which can be used to predict and explain other people's behaviour is known as what?

   A. Theory of mind.

   B. Metacognition.

   C. Chunking.

   D. Encoding.

Your answer: ☐

Advanced level questions

15. Danielle is a primary school teacher who wants her class to achieve the best that they can. According to Piaget, how could she encourage their development?

   A. Create situations that enable discovery learning.

   B. Provide one-on-one tutoring for each of her pupils.

   C. Involve older pupils to act as mentors for her pupils.

   D. Reinforce correct answers and ignore wrong ones.

Your answer: ☐

16. Five-year-old Hannah is attempting to complete Piaget's three mountain task and is asked to choose the picture that shows 'what the doll sees'. According to Piaget, Hannah will do which of the following?

A. Choose the picture that the doll sees, the correct picture.

B. Select the picture that shows her perspective.

C. Select the correct picture but be unable to explain why she chose it.

D. Be unable to decide which picture is correct.

Your answer:

17. Naomi is 2 years old and tells you that there aren't any boats on the lake because they're all asleep. This is an example of what?

A. Inductive reasoning.

B. Centration.

C. Animism.

D. Egocentrism.

Your answer:

18. Javid is 6 years old and is shown two identical jars of water which are both tall and thin. The researcher takes one of these glasses and empties it into a third glass which is short and wide. According to Piaget, Javid will state what?

A. The shorter glass will contain more water.

B. The researcher took some water away.

C. The glasses contain the same amount of water.

D. The tall thin glass has more water.

Your answer:

19. During the conservation task, the focus on one specific detail such as the height of the glass rather than on the dimensions of the glass is known as what?

A. Conservation.

B. Centration.

C. Irreversibility.

D. Depth perception.

Your answer:

20. Ziona's mother is trying to wean her from her dummy. While 1-year-old Ziona is watching, her mother puts her dummy in a drawer and covers it with a blanket. She then moves the dummy to a different location. Ziona will do which of the following?

    A. Look for her dummy in the original hiding place.

    B. Be unable to find her dummy unless she finds it by accident.

    C. Successfully locate her dummy in the new location.

    D. Not try to find her dummy.

Your answer: ☐

21. Which of the following is not a criticism of Piaget's theory of development?

    A. His concepts such as assimilation and accommodation are too vague to be of any use.

    B. Cognitive development may not occur in the sequence proposed by Piaget.

    C. Development may not occur in a domain general fashion.

    D. Children cannot actually perform the tasks Piaget set.

Your answer: ☐

22. The major distinction between Piaget and Vygotsky is that Vygotsky placed greater emphasis on what?

    A. The impact of biological factors on development.

    B. Social interaction with other children and caregivers.

    C. The role of age-based stages.

    D. The need for reinforcement of behaviours.

Your answer: ☐

23. Vygotsky believed that private speech has which of the following characteristics?

    A. It changes in form as children grow older.

    B. It greatly improves children's ability to complete problem-solving tasks.

    C. It is a method of regulating behaviour.

    D. All of the above.

Your answer: ☐

24. Laura is a school teacher. She introduces a mentoring scheme in which older pupils help younger ones with any issues that they may experience at school. This is an example of what?

A. Reciprocal teaching.

B. Scaffolding.

C. Cooperative learning.

D. Reciprocity.

Your answer:

25. A small group of children are working together on their science project. Some of the group are better at science than others. This is an example of what?

A. Reciprocal teaching.

B. Scaffolding.

C. Cooperative learning.

D. Reciprocity.

Your answer:

26. Aisha is asked to read a list of words and then recall as many as she can. Aisha decides to group similar words together. This is an example of which memory strategy?

A. Elaboration.

B. Organisation.

C. Rehearsal.

D. Association.

Your answer:

27. Seven-year-old Millie is learning her 8 times table. Her teacher tells her that the best way to help her remember is by repeating them to herself. Which memory strategy is Millie using?

A. Organisation.

B. Rehearsal.

C. Elaboration.

D. Chunking.

Your answer:

28. A researcher is interested in examining the impact that children's awareness of memory strategies has on how much they remember. Which phenomenon is the researcher studying?

A. Cognitive self-regulation.

B. Meta cognition.

C. Academic self-efficiency.

D. Phonological awareness.

Your answer: ☐

Extended multiple-choice question

Complete the following paragraph using the items listed below. Not all of the items will be needed and each item can only be used once.

The _____ views cognitive development as an analogy between the computer and the human mind. Information processing theories share three basic assumptions. The first is that _____ such as _____ are a form of information processing. Secondly, information processing theories emphasise _____ that move development from one state to the next. The third assumption is _____, the idea that previous knowledge can modify thinking and facilitate higher levels of cognitive development. Siegler (1998) suggested that information processing theories emphasise the _____ and _____ that provide mechanisms for the adaptation of cognition to environmental influences. These structural characteristics include stores such as a _____, _____ and _____. Processes include _____ and _____. More recently, information processing research has expanded to include _____ incorporating psychology, biology, neuroscience and medicine to advance our understanding of the relationship between changes in the brain, cognitive processing and behaviour.

Optional items

A. automisation

B. change mechanisms

C. developmental cognitive neuroscience

(continued overleaf)

D. encoding

E. information processing approach

F. long-term memory

G. neuropsychology

H. processes

I. remembering

J. thought processes

K. self-modification

L. sensory register

M. stores

N. structural characteristics

O. schemas

P. working memory

Essay questions for Chapter 7

Once you have completed the MCQs above you are ready to tackle some essay questions. You might like to select three or four topics and make notes on them. One way of doing this is to create a concept map. The first question has been done for you and you can see how the knowledge required links to some of the MCQs in this chapter.

1. Compare and contrast both Piaget's and Vygotsky's theories of cognitive development.

2. With reference to research examining the development of object permanence in infancy, discuss the implications for the validity of Piaget's sensorimotor stage of development.

3. With reference to research evidence, evaluate the extent to which cognitive development occurs according to stages proposed by Piaget.

4. Discuss how Vygotsky's notion of the zone of proximal development expands our understanding of early cognitive development.

5. Critically evaluate how Vygotsky's theory can be applied to the field of education.

6. To what extent can Vygotsky's notion of scaffolding be applied across the lifespan?

7. Describe and evaluate how information processing theory has advanced our understanding of cognitive development.

8. Discuss the extent to which using a computer metaphor fails to account for the complexities of cognitive development.

Chapter 7 essay question 1: concept map

Compare and contrast both Piaget's and Vygotsky's theories of cognitive development.

The concept map below provides an example of the topic areas that you might include when writing your essay. Remember that it is important to link your answers to other topic areas not covered in this chapter. This question requires you to describe and evaluate two key theories of cognitive development. Good answers to this question will not only discuss the strengths and weaknesses of these theories but consider the stance of these theorists on human development and illustrate this with examples from a variety of topic areas.

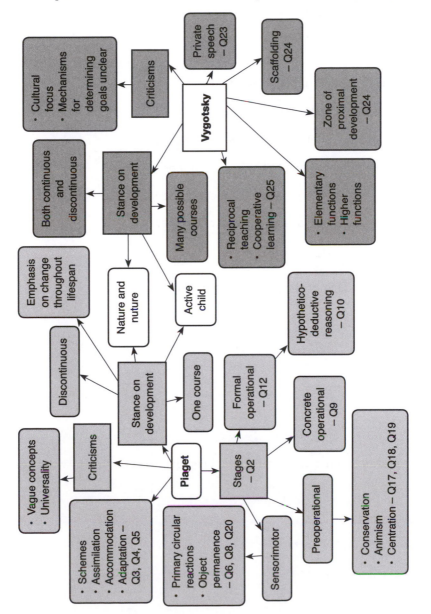

Chapter 8
Moral development

This chapter provides questions relating to the foundations of morality (e.g. the psychoanalytic perspective and social learning theory), Piaget's theory of moral development, Kohlberg's theory of moral development, sex differences in moral reasoning, influences on moral development and moral behaviour.

Select one of the possible answers for each question.

Foundation level questions

1. Moral development is thought to reflect what?

    A. Biological, emotional and cognitive components.

    B. Cognitive, emotional and behavioural components.

    C. Biological, cultural and behavioural components.

    D. Behavioural, emotional and cultural components.

Your answer: ☐

2. According to Freud, moral development is guided by what?

    A. The id.

    B. The ego.

    C. The superego.

    D. The libido.

Your answer: ☐

3. Freud believed that moral development was largely complete by what age?

    A. 5–6 years.

    B. Adolescence.

    C. Between 7 and 11 years.

    D. Between 2 and 4 years.

Your answer: ☐

4. According to learning theorists, morality develops through what?

   A. Stages determined by cognitive ability.

   B. Identifying with the same-sex parent.

   C. Inductive discipline.

   D. Learning processes.

Your answer: ☐

5. Piaget's theory of moral development consists of the _____ stage and the _____ stage.

   A. Premoral, post moral.

   B. Moral realism, moral relativism.

   C. Preconventional, postconventional.

   D. Amoral, postmoral.

Your answer: ☐

6. Which research method did Piaget use to study the development of children's moral thinking?

   A. Clinical interviews.

   B. Questionnaires.

   C. Laboratory experiments.

   D. Ethnography.

Your answer: ☐

7. Piaget believed that rigidity in children's development in the moral realism stage was due to what?

   A. Reciprocity.

   B. Conservation.

   C. Egocentrism.

   D. Assimilation.

Your answer: ☐

8. What did Kohlberg use to test his theory of moral development?

    A. Clinical interviews with children.

    B. Three mountains task.

    C. Moral judgement interview.

    D. Modelling behaviour.

Your answer: ☐

9. Which of the following shows Kohlberg's stages of moral development in the correct order?

    A. Preconventional, conventional, postconventional.

    B. Premoral, moral realism, moral relativism.

    C. Amoral, premoral, post moral.

    D. Premoral, conventional, post moral.

Your answer: ☐

10. Gilligan criticised Kohlberg's theory of moral development for what reason?

    A. His interviews were only conducted with males and so did not represent the morality of girls and women.

    B. The theory failed to account for cultural influences.

    C. The theory failed to emphasise an 'ethic of care'.

    D. Both A and C.

Your answer: ☐

11. Turiel's domain theory emphasises the distinction between which two concepts?

    A. Morality and social convention.

    B. Morality and justice.

    C. Social norms and morality of care.

    D. Morality and cognitive development.

Your answer: ☐

12. According to Turiel, moral actions are concerned with what?

    A. A child's understanding of social organisation.

    B. The effect upon the well-being of a person.

    C. The existence of social norms.

    D. The functioning of social groups.

    Your answer: ☐

Advanced level questions

13. Siobhan hits her younger brother Matthew around the face. Siobhan and Matthew's parents take Siobhan aside and explain to her that hitting her brother is unacceptable behaviour and tell her she is not allowed to go outside to play tomorrow. This strategy is known as what?

    A. Power assertion.

    B. Inductive discipline.

    C. Privilege withdrawal.

    D. Responsive parenting.

    Your answer: ☐

14. In response to the Heinz dilemma, John states: 'Heinz should steal the drug because he is a good man who wants to save his wife's life.' According to Kohlberg, John is at which level and stage?

    A. Level 2, stage 1.

    B. Level 3, stage 2.

    C. Level 1, stage 2.

    D. Level 2, stage 2.

    Your answer: ☐

15. In response to the Heinz dilemma, Reeta states: 'Heinz should do everything he can to save his wife and show her compassion. Respect for human life is far more important than material things.' This illustrates which of the following?

A. Social contact orientation.

B. Universal ethical principle orientation.

C. Maintenance of social order.

D. Instrumental orientation.

Your answer:

16. Anna desperately wants to open her Christmas presents and knows where her parents have hidden them but manages to resist the temptation. Anna is engaging in what?

A. Conventional morality.

B. Moral reasoning.

C. A delay of gratification.

D. Moral relativism.

Your answer:

17. Children who can understand the perspectives of others are more likely to show what?

A. Sympathy.

B. Prosocial behaviour.

C. Guilt.

D. Altruism.

Your answer:

18. Parenting strategies that involve power assertion, physical punishment, love withdrawal and inconsistent discipline have been associated with what?

A. Antisocial behaviour in both sexes.

B. Prosocial behaviour in males.

C. Antisocial behaviour in males.

D. Antisocial behaviour in males more than females.

Your answer:

19. Malika is asked how she would split up the profits made from the cake stall at the school fete. Malika replies, 'Laura should get the most because she sold the most cakes.' How old is Malika?

A. 4–5.

B. 9–10.

C. 6–8.

D. 5–7.

Your answer:

20. Susan is asked how she would divide a bag of sweets among her friends. Susan says, 'Everyone should have the same number of sweets because that's only fair.' This is an example of which stage in the development of distributive justice?

A. Stage 1.

B. Stage 2.

C. Stage 3.

D. Both stage 2 and 3.

Your answer:

21. Deepak pushes Asif out of the way so that he can be first in line in the school dinner queue. This is an example of which type of aggression?

A. Hostile.

B. Instrumental.

C. Hedonistic.

D. Cognitive.

Your answer:

22. Felicity posts a series of derogatory comments about the company she works for on a social networking site. This is a type of what?

A. Relational aggression.

B. Verbal aggression.

C. Hedonism.

D. Instrumental aggression.

Your answer:

23. Crick and Dodge (1994) proposed that aggression develops due to which of the following factors?

    A. Environmental causes.

    B. Genetic factors.

    C. Changes in cognitive development.

    D. How social cognitions are processed.

Your answer:

24. Which of the following factors outside of the family context may contribute to the development of aggression?

    A. Lack of sense of community.

    B. Children who become friends with others who display aggressive behaviour.

    C. Large class sizes.

    D. Both B and C.

Your answer:

Extended multiple-choice question

Complete the following paragraph using the items listed opposite. Not all of the items will be needed and each item can only be used once.

Research has indicated that _____ also plays an important role in moral development, specifically in moral behaviour. Emotions such as gratitude, guilt and love can mediate the relationship between moral thought and behaviour. Moral action can be expressed through _____ while immoral action can typically involve _____. Gains in prosocial behaviour have been attributed to changes in _____, emotional understanding and the child's _____. Research examining the development of prosocial behaviour has identified that it is _____ over time; children who are kind and considerate at _____ are likely to remain so at _____. Consequently, behaviour in early childhood is regarded as a strong predictor of behaviour in later development. Evidence from _____ has highlighted the role of genes in the development of prosocial behaviour; however, the contribution of _____ is also important.

Optional items

A. adolescence

B. age 7

C. age 14

D. aggression

E. changeable

F. cognitive development

G. distributive justice

H. emotion

I. environment

J. environmental factors

K. gratification

L. infancy

M. laboratory studies

N. physical development

O. prosocial behaviour

P. stable

Q. twin studies

Essay questions for Chapter 8

Once you have completed the MCQs above you are ready to tackle some essay questions. You might like to select three or four topics and make notes on them. One way of doing this is to create a concept map. The first question has been done for you and you can see how the knowledge required links to some of the MCQs in this chapter.

1. Critically discuss how moral reasoning may impact on the development of moral behaviour.

2. Discuss why Piaget's theory of moral development is considered an inadequate explanation in the development of morality.

3. Critically discuss how learning theory can be used to inform the development of positive parenting programmes.

4. With reference to research literature, describe and evaluate four factors that may influence the development of moral reasoning.

5. Discuss the extent to which genetics and the environment account for the development of prosocial behaviour.

6. Discuss factors that may contribute to sex differences in the development of aggression between early childhood and adolescence.

7. With reference to research and theory, discuss interventions aimed at tackling behavioural problems in children and young people.

8. Critically analyse the claim that sex differences in moral reasoning can be attributed to typical gender roles.

Chapter 8 essay question 1: concept map

Critically discuss how moral reasoning may impact on the development of moral behaviour.

The concept map below provides an example of the topic areas that you might include when writing your essay. Remember that it is important to link your answers to other topic areas not covered in this chapter. This question requires you to describe and evaluate the relationship between moral reasoning and moral behaviour. Good answers to this question will discuss both prosocial and anti-social behaviour and consider the importance of genetic, enviromental and socio-cultural factors on moral development.

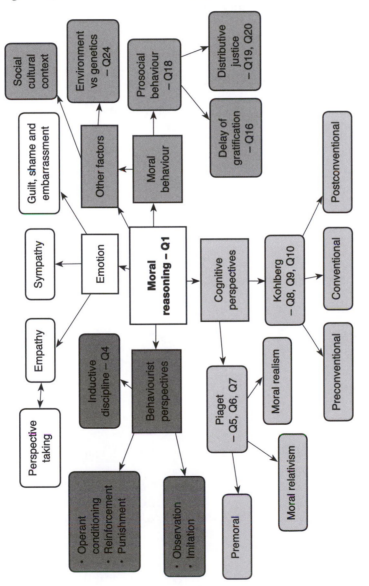

Chapter 9
Identity development

This chapter provides questions relating to self-awareness during infancy, the development of self-concept and self-esteem throughout childhood, influences on self-esteem, changes in self-concept and self-esteem during adolescence, adolescence as a period of storm and stress and identity status.

Select one of the possible answers for each question.

Foundation level questions

1. The development of self-awareness begins at what age?

    A. First few months of life.

    B. 1–2 years.

    C. 2–3 years.

    D. 3–4 years.

    Your answer:

2. At what age do children become consciously aware of the self's physical features?

    A. First few months of life.

    B. 12 months.

    C. 24 months.

    D. 36 months.

    Your answer:

3. What test do researchers use to test self-recognition in infants?

    A. The rouge test.

    B. Rorschach test.

    C. IQ test.

    D. Attitude test.

    Your answer:

4. Which of the following have researchers not used to study self-recognition?

   A. Mirrors.

   B. Photographs.

   C. Videotape.

   D. Audiotape.

Your answer: ☐

5. Self-awareness in infancy has been associated with the development of what?

   A. Self-esteem and empathy.

   B. Empathy and compliance.

   C. Compliance and self-esteem.

   D. Delay of gratification.

Your answer: ☐

6. Between 18 and 30 months children begin to develop what?

   A. Social referencing.

   B. Social comparisons.

   C. A categorical self.

   D. Self-concept.

Your answer: ☐

7. What cues used by infants suggest self-recognition?

   A. Visual.

   B. Featural.

   C. Contingency.

   D. Non-contingency.

Your answer: ☐

8. If a toddler can pass the mirror task then they are not likely to display what?

    A. Empathy.

    B. Egocentrism.

    C. Prosocial behaviour.

    D. Imitative play.

Your answer: ☐

9. Which researcher first proposed a developmental sequence of children's self-descriptions?

    A. Piaget.

    B. Freud.

    C. Harter.

    D. Erikson.

Your answer: ☐

10. Which research method did Rosenberg (1979) use in his study of children's self-descriptions?

    A. Interviews.

    B. Case studies.

    C. Laboratory experiments.

    D. Ethnography.

Your answer: ☐

11. Rosenberg (1979) used which set of terms for his broad groups of self-descriptions?

    A. Physical, cultural, social, psychological.

    B. Physical, character, inner, relationships.

    C. Character, inner, personality, social.

    D. Inner, relationships, personality, objective facts.

Your answer: ☐

12. Rosenberg found that the majority of the descriptions given by younger children were about _____. Older children were more likely to use _____ to define the self.

   A. Physical characteristics, character traits.

   B. Character traits, physical characteristics.

   C. Inner qualities, character traits.

   D. Character traits, inner qualities.

Your answer: ☐

13. Social comparisons lead to the development of what?

   A. The categorical self.

   B. The physical self.

   C. The ideal self.

   D. The academic self.

Your answer: ☐

14. Cross-cultural research has indicated what about the development of the self-concept?

   A. It is predetermined by genetics.

   B. It does not follow the same trajectory in all societies.

   C. It is absent in certain cultures.

   D. It appears to be universal to all children.

Your answer: ☐

15. Which of the following psychologists first proposed that adolescence is ultimately a period of storm and stress?

   A. G. Stanley Hall.

   B. Anna Freud.

   C. Margaret Mead.

   D. Sigmund Freud.

Your answer: ☐

Advanced level questions

16. Which of the following is not a traditional feature of storm and stress in adolescence?

    A. Higher rates of antisocial behaviour.

    B. Resistance to adult authority.

    C. Increased mood swings.

    D. Issues with self-image.

Your answer: ☐

17. Lucy, 15, comments, 'Some people wear their hearts on their sleeves but I don't show my feelings.' According to Rosenberg, Lucy is using what type of self-description?

    A. Physical.

    B. Character.

    C. Relationships.

    D. Inner.

Your answer: ☐

18. Chantelle frequently tells her daughter, 'You're fantastic', even though she hasn't done anything to deserve praise. According to Damon her daughter will do what?

    A. Develop high self-esteem.

    B. Begin to doubt herself.

    C. Accept her opinion without doubt.

    D. Develop learned helplessness.

Your answer: ☐

19. Alison failed her end-of-year maths test. She tells you that the reason she failed was because she didn't put in enough effort. This is an example of what?

    A. Social comparison.

    B. Learned helplessness.

    C. A mastery-orientated attribution.

    D. Problem-centred coping.

Your answer: ☐

20. Claire comments, 'The reason I failed my exam is because I'm just not clever enough.' Claire is demonstrating what?

    A. Social comparison.

    B. Learned helplessness.

    C. A mastery-orientated attribution.

    D. Problem-centred coping.

Your answer:

21. Elliott's IQ is much higher than Shami's but Shami typically achieves better grades on her assignments. Which of the following is the most likely explanation for this?

    A. Elliott has a high achievement identity.

    B. The IQ test was not valid.

    C. Elliott has low self-esteem.

    D. Shami has developed high achievement motivation.

Your answer:

22. Which type of parenting is associated with higher levels of self-esteem?

    A. Authoritative.

    B. Authoritarian.

    C. Permissive.

    D. Neglectful.

Your answer:

23. A teacher sets up an intervention to encourage children who display learned helplessness that they can overcome failure by exerting more effort. This is known as what?

    A. Attribution retraining.

    B. Reciprocal teaching.

    C. Coaching.

    D. Mentoring.

Your answer:

24. Katzu is Japanese and Connor is American. How is their self-esteem likely to differ?

  A. Connor will score lower in self-esteem than Katzu.

  B. Katzu will score lower in self-esteem than Connor.

  C. Self-esteem will be similar for both children.

  D. Katzu is more likely to feel less confident about his academic ability.

Your answer: ☐

25. When asked about future career choices, Olivia replies, 'Having explored a lot of options, I know a career in medicine is definitely for me.' Olivia is demonstrating:

  A. Identity achievement.

  B. Identity moratorium.

  C. Identity foreclosure.

  D. Identity diffusion.

Your answer: ☐

26. Kwame is uncertain about what he wants to do in life and feels overwhelmed about making important life choices. Kwame is experiencing what?

  A. Identity achievement.

  B. Identity moratorium.

  C. Identity foreclosure.

  D. Identity diffusion.

Your answer: ☐

27. An individual who displays identity moratorium is likely to show which of the following characteristics?

  A. Lack clear direction, be uncommitted to values and goals and feel overwhelmed.

  B. Commit themselves to values and goals without exploring alternatives.

  C. Have not made firm commitments and be in the process of trying out activities to discover values and goals to guide their lives.

  D. Have already explored alternatives and be committed to a clearly formulated set of values and goals.

Your answer: ☐

28. James states that he accepts his parents' views on the existence of God without question. Which identity status is James likely to have?

   A. Diffused.

   B. Foreclosed.

   C. Achieved.

   D. Moratorium.

Your answer: ☐

29. Which two identity statuses are likely to use an information-gathering cognitive style?

   A. Achieved, moratorium.

   B. Foreclosed, diffused.

   C. Diffused, achieved.

   D. Moratorium, foreclosed.

Your answer: ☐

30. Adolescents who experience time management and academic difficulties typically use which type of cognitive style?

   A. Information gathering.

   B. Dogmatic inflexible.

   C. Dogmatic flexible.

   D. Diffuse avoidant.

Your answer: ☐

Extended multiple-choice question

Complete the following paragraphs using the items listed below and opposite. Not all of the items will be needed and each item can only be used once.

In 1904 _____ proposed that adolescence is essentially a period of storm and stress, a period of psychological turmoil. This comprised three specific characteristics:_____, conflict with parents and _____. Hall adopted a _____ perspective suggesting that evolution occurs when organisms pass on their characteristics from one generation to the next, not in the form of genes but in the form of experiences and acquired characteristics.

However, _____ (1928) argued that not all groups will show signs of a 'tumultuous' period; rather it represents a _____ transition from childhood to adolescence. _____ proposed that not all adolescents experience storm and stress; rather, adolescence is a period when storm and stress is _____ to occur. Parental warmth, _____ and establishing autonomy are vital factors in emotional development; absence of _____, whether physical or verbal, may result in symptoms of storm and stress. The rise of _____ is also thought to be a contributing factor.

Optional items

A. Arnett

B. conflict

C. Darwinian

D. engagement in risk-taking behaviours

E. Erikson

F. globalisation

G. gradual

H. G. Stanley Hall

I. Lamarckian evolutionary

J. low self-esteem

K. Margaret Mead

L. mood disruption

M. more likely

N. parental warmth

O. rapid

P. self-concept

Q. Valliant

Essay questions for Chapter 9

Once you have completed the MCQs above you are ready to tackle some essay questions. You might like to select three or four topics and make notes on them. One way of doing this is to create a concept map. The first question has been done for you and you can see how the knowledge required links to some of the MCQs in this chapter.

1. Discuss how the development of self-awareness in infancy impacts upon emotional and social development.

2. Discuss how learned helplessness can influence self-esteem during middle childhood.

3. Compare and contrast how self-concept and self-esteem change between middle childhood and adolescence.

4. To what extent can changes in sense of self be explained by Rosenberg's study of self-descriptions? What other developmental changes may these reflect?

5. Discuss the extent to which adolescence can be defined as a period of 'storm and stress'.

6. Critically evaluate the factors that may affect identity development during adolescence.

7. Discuss how the lifespan model of development can be applied to the development of self-esteem.

8. Evaluate the impact of early negative experiences on the development of self-esteem in adolescence.

Chapter 9 essay question 1: concept map

Discuss how the development of self-awareness in infancy impacts upon emotional and social development.

The concept map below provides an example of the topic areas that you might include when writing your essay. Remember that it is important to link your answers to other topic areas not covered in this chapter. This question requires you to describe and evaluate the impact of the development of self-awareness on emotional and social development. Good answers to this question will draw upon issues concerning perceptual development (Chapter 3), specifically the role of intermodal perception on self-awareness, and development of moral behaviour (Chapter 8), e.g. self-control and compliance.

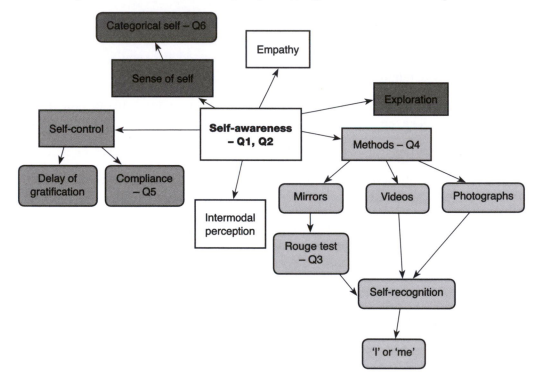

Chapter 10
Adulthood

This chapter provides questions relating to cognitive development during adulthood, physical changes and emotional development including theories of psychosocial development.

Select one of the possible answers for each question.

Foundation level questions

1. Emerging adulthood typically occurs between what ages?

   A. 18–25 years.

   B. 20–25 years.

   C. 26–30 years.

   D. 30+ years.

   Your answer:

2. Which of the following is not a feature of emerging adulthood?

   A. A time of exploration including changes in educational paths and jobs.

   B. Peer groups become organised around cliques.

   C. Becoming increasingly self-focused.

   D. Increased optimism about the future.

   Your answer:

3. What factors have contributed to the concept of emerging adulthood?

   A. Changes in physical development.

   B. Changes in cognitive development.

   C. Social norms and expectations.

   D. Increased dependence on parents.

   Your answer:

4. The peak of physical fitness occurs during which phase of adulthood?

   A. Early.

   B. Early to middle.

   C. Middle.

   D. Middle to late.

Your answer: ☐

5. Physical changes become most apparent between what ages?

   A. 25–30.

   B. 30–35.

   C. 35–40.

   D. 40 and above.

Your answer: ☐

6. Which of the following physical changes is not likely to emerge during late adulthood?

   A. Sensitivity to sound declines, especially at high frequencies.

   B. Reduced ability to detect and identify odours.

   C. Hair greys and thins.

   D. Decreased elasticity in the skin.

Your answer: ☐

7. Who provided the starting point for the growing research literature on the development of epistemic growth?

   A. Levinson.

   B. Valliant.

   C. Perry.

   D. Erikson.

Your answer: ☐

8. Which of the following is not a feature of Perry's theory of epistemic cognition?

   A. Dualistic thinking.

   B. Relativistic thinking.

   C. Commitment within relativistic thinking.

   D. Formal operation thought.

Your answer: ☐

9. Peer interaction during early adulthood may result in advances in what?

   A. Metacognition.

   B. Peer acceptance.

   C. Pragmatic thought.

   D. Expertise.

Your answer: ☐

10. During early adulthood, which period of vocational development is an individual likely to be in?

   A. Fantasy.

   B. Tentative.

   C. Realistic.

   D. Optimistic.

Your answer: ☐

11. Information processing speed is thought to do which of the following?

   A. Increase during middle adulthood.

   B. Decrease during middle adulthood.

   C. Reach its peak in middle adulthood .

   D. Decline during early adulthood.

Your answer: ☐

12. The midlife transition in which fertility decreases is known as what?

   A. The climacteric.

   B. Presbyopia.

   C. Presbycusis.

   D. Menopause.

Your answer: ☐

13. During middle adulthood, _____ intelligence steadily increases while _____ intelligence decreases.

   A. Fluid, crystallised.

   B. Crystallised, fluid.

   C. Relativistic, epistemic.

   D. Epistemic, relativistic.

Your answer: ☐

14. Continued growth in middle adulthood may take which form?

   A. Peer interaction and reflection.

   B. Increased wisdom.

   C. Practical problem-solving.

   D. Pragmatic thought.

Your answer: ☐

15. Which of the following is not a physical change likely to emerge in late adulthood?

   A. Increase in body fat on the torso.

   B. Decrease in height.

   C. Decrease in sensitivity to taste.

   D. Fertility problems.

Your answer: ☐

Advanced level questions

16. Levinson's theory emphasised the importance of what?

    A. Overcoming psychological conflict.

    B. The development of pragmatic thought.

    C. Life structures.

    D. Epistemic growth.

    Your answer:

17. According to Erikson, what is the major conflict likely to be present in early adulthood?

    A. Identity versus role confusion.

    B. Intimacy versus isolation.

    C. Generativity versus stagnation.

    D. Ego integrity versus despair.

    Your answer:

18. Louise is in her early 30s. According to Valliant's theory, Louise is likely to focus on what?

    A. Career consolidation.

    B. Establishing intimacy.

    C. Guiding others.

    D. Spiritual reflection.

    Your answer:

19. Which of the following is not a major limitation of Levinson's theory?

    A. It was based on interviews conducted in the first few decades of the twentieth century.

    B. The sample consisted of mostly college-educated men.

    C. It failed to account for the impact of low socio-economic status.

    D. It provides only a broad sketch of personality development.

    Your answer:

20. Which of the following is not likely to be associated with positive psychological well-being in early adulthood?

   A. Warm sibling relationships.

   B. Lack of gratifying friendships.

   C. Resistant attachment during childhood.

   D. Secure attachment during childhood.

Your answer:

21. Julia is 40 years of age and after devoting the past ten years to raising her children has decided that she wants to focus on rebuilding her career. This is an example of which of Levinson's four developmental tasks?

   A. Young–old.

   B. Destruction–creation.

   C. Masculinity–femininity.

   D. Engagement–separateness.

Your answer:

22. Maria is in her mid-40s and has recently been promoted at work. Her work colleagues have noticed that she has become more assertive. Which of Levinson's developmental tasks does this reflect?

   A. Young–old.

   B. Destruction–creation.

   C. Masculinity–femininity.

   D. Engagement–separateness.

Your answer:

23. Iqbal tells you that when he was 25 he was offered the opportunity to study for a doctoral degree which he did not accept and now regrets. However, in his 40s he decided to pursue his earlier desire to study for a higher degree. Iqbal is likely to display what?

   A. Favourable psychological well-being and poorer physical health.

   B. Favourable psychological well-being and good physical health.

   C. Less favourable psychological well-being and poor physical health.

   D. Less favourable psychological well-being and good physical health.

Your answer:

24. Rochelle, who is 43 years old, is organising a garden party for the whole family to celebrate her daughter's 21st birthday. Rochelle has taken on which of the following roles?

   A. Kinkeeper.

   B. Valued elder.

   C. Mentor.

   D. Nurturer.

Your answer:

25. Joy and Judith are sisters, both in their 50s. How is their contact likely to have changed from when they were in early adulthood?

   A. Contact will be the same as when they were younger.

   B. Contact will have increased.

   C. Contact will have decreased.

   D. Contact will increase briefly but decrease as they approach 60.

Your answer:

26. Jackie has just retired after a long career in the police force. She is now thinking of other things that will give her the same satisfaction she experienced in her job. According to Peck, which task is Jackie engaging in?

   A. Body transcendence versus body preoccupation.

   B. Ego transcendence versus ego preoccupation.

   C. Affect optimisation.

   D. Ego differentiation versus work-role preoccupation.

   Your answer: ☐

27. Henry maintains that despite failing health, he is generally optimistic about life. Henry has developed what characteristic?

   A. Affect optimisation.

   B. Reminiscence.

   C. Ego integrity.

   D. Body preoccupation.

   Your answer: ☐

28. Which of the following is the least likely function of elder friendship?

   A. Intimacy and companionship.

   B. Acceptance.

   C. Protection from the psychological consequences of loss.

   D. To bolster self-worth and importance.

   Your answer: ☐

29. Joan is a member of her local bowls club which she attends once a week. Attending the club is likely to provide Joan with what?

   A. Primary friends.

   B. Secondary friends.

   C. Intimate friends.

   D. Practical assistance.

   Your answer: ☐

30. On leaving a coffee shop Elaine asks, 'Where's your walking stick, Eileen? 'Don't be embarrassed, I'll need one before you know it.' What function of elder friendship does this illustrate?

A. Intimacy and companionship.

B. Acceptance.

C. Protection from the psychological consequences of loss.

D. Links to the community.

Your answer: ☐

Extended multiple-choice question

Despite increased life expectancy retirement remains an inevitable process towards the end of middle adulthood. Henry is a surgical specialist who is about to reach his 57th birthday and is debating whether he should retire or continue working. To help him make up his mind, you encourage him to write down a list of factors that may influence his decision. Sort the items listed below into either the 'Retire' or 'Continue working' category. On the basis of this, what should Henry do?

Retire	Continue working

Optional items

A. Good pension

B. Financially secure

C. Flexible working

D. Health problems

E. Reached highest point in profession

(continued overleaf)

F. Spend more time on the golf course

G. Spend more time with the grandchildren

H. Rewarding job

I. Spouse due to retire

J. Stimulating work environment

Essay questions for Chapter 10

Once you have completed the MCQs above you are ready to tackle some essay questions. You might like to select three or four topics and make notes on them. One way of doing this is to create a concept map. The first question has been done for you and you can see how the knowledge required links to some of the MCQs in this chapter.

1. Discuss what is meant by emerging adulthood and how cultural changes have influenced the emergence of this period.

2. Describe and evaluate gender differences in the process of ageing.

3. Describe how cognitive abilities may change during adulthood and evaluate the debate about when these changes are likely to occur.

4. Analyse the extent to which crises experienced during adulthood are different to those experienced during adolescence. What does this suggest about the nature of development?

5. Critically evaluate the relationship between physical ageing and psychological well-being in adulthood.

6. Discuss how relationships change during adulthood and the impact of this on psychological adjustment to ageing.

7. Compare and contrast Levinson's seasons of life theory with Valliant's adaptations to life theory.

8. Critically reflect upon the extent to which the midlife crisis is an inevitable feature of adulthood.

Chapter 10 essay question 1: concept map

Discuss what is meant by emerging adulthood and how cultural changes have influenced the emergence of this period.

The concept map below provides an example of the topic areas that you might include when writing your essay. Remember that it is important to link your answers to other topic areas not covered in this chapter. This question requires you to describe the concept of emerging adulthood and evaluate the role of cultural factors and social norms and expectations on this period of developtment. It is important that you illustrate your answer with examples and make reference to developmental theories, particularly the lifespan model of development which emphasises the multiple interacting forces which influence development.

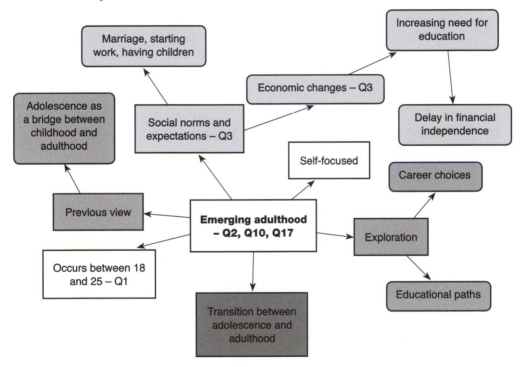

Chapter 11
Death, dying and bereavement

This chapter provides questions relating to defining death, age-related attitudes towards death, stages of dying, end-of-life care, euthanasia and suicide, and coping with death.

Select one of the possible answers for each question.

Foundation level questions

1. The stage where the individual passes into permanent death is known as what?

    A. Agonal.

    B. Clinical death.

    C. Mortality.

    D. Vegetative.

    Your answer: ☐

2. What is the *contemporary* definition of death in western societies?

    A. Loss of vital signs, e.g. heartbeat and respiration.

    B. The irreversible cessation of brain and brain stem activity.

    C. Persistent vegetative state.

    D. Loss of respiration.

    Your answer: ☐

3. The state in which the brain stem remains active but the cerebral cortex no longer registers electrical activity is known as what?

    A. Brain death.

    B. Cerebral death.

    C. Persistent vegetative state.

    D. Neural decline.

    Your answer: ☐

4. Death anxiety is more widespread among which group?

   A. Young children.

   B. Adolescents.

   C. Young adults.

   D. Middle-aged adults.

   Your answer:

5. In western culture, what has research suggested limits death anxiety?

   A. Religion.

   B. A sense of life's meaning.

   C. Fear of the body decaying.

   D. The number of people a person has lost.

   Your answer:

6. Why might death anxiety reach its lowest point in late adulthood?

   A. Older adults have developed ego integrity.

   B. Elders have attained symbolic immortality.

   C. Older adults are more religious than younger adults.

   D. Both A and B.

   Your answer:

7. Which of the following might lead children to express death anxiety?

   A. If they live in high-crime areas.

   B. If they live in war-torn areas.

   C. If they are terminally ill.

   D. All of the above.

   Your answer:

8. Research has shown that which of the following is true, regardless of age and culture?

A. Women are more anxious about death than men.

B. Men are more anxious about death than women.

C. Men and women are equally as anxious about death.

D. Women are only more anxious about the death of their spouse.

Your answer: ☐

9. Death anxiety in adulthood has been shown to be related to what?

A. Physical health.

B. Mental health.

C. Both physical and mental health in equal amounts.

D. Physical health slightly more than mental health.

Your answer: ☐

10. The withholding or withdrawal of life-sustaining treatment allowing a patient to die naturally is known as what?

A. Assisted suicide.

B. Voluntary active euthanasia.

C. Involuntary active euthanasia.

D. Voluntary passive euthanasia.

Your answer: ☐

11. Kübler-Ross's (1969) theory emphasised the role of which of the following?

A. Psychological needs of dying patients.

B. Social needs of dying patients.

C. Cultural aspects of death.

D. Clinical features of death.

Your answer: ☐

12. Kübler-Ross's theory is comprised of how many stages?

    A. 3.

    B. 4.

    C. 5.

    D. 6.

Your answer: ☐

13. Which of the following shows Kübler-Ross's stages of dying in the correct order?

    A. Anger, denial, bargaining, depression, acceptance, readjustment.

    B. Denial, anger, bargaining, depression, acceptance.

    C. Anger, denial, depression, bargaining, acceptance.

    D. Denial, depression, anger, bargaining, acceptance, transition.

Your answer: ☐

14. Which of the following is a criticism of Kübler-Ross's theory?

    A. The stages are too limited.

    B. They do not extend to all cultures.

    C. Individuals may not move through the stages in a specified sequence.

    D. Both A and C.

Your answer: ☐

15. Which of the following is *not* a feature of an appropriate death?

    A. As free from suffering as possible.

    B. Maintains and enhances significant relationships.

    C. A death that is anticipated.

    D. Makes sense in terms of the individual's living pattern.

Your answer: ☐

Advanced level questions

16. Martin has liver failure. He signs a written statement authorising his wife to make healthcare decisions on his behalf should his health deteriorate further. This is an example of what?

  A. A medical will.

  B. A living directive.

  C. An advanced power of attorney.

  D. A durable power of attorney.

Your answer: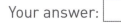

17. Which of the following is not a feature of hospice care?

  A. Care is provided by an interdisciplinary team.

  B. Emphasis is placed on the patient's physical care.

  C. Emphasis on palliative care.

  D. Follow-up bereavement services for families in the year following a death.

Your answer:

18. Which of the following is not a feature of hospital dying?

  A. The patient and family as a unit of care.

  B. The physical state of the dying person.

  C. The goal and quality of the care.

  D. The unit in which dying occurs.

Your answer:

19. In which setting would you typically expect family members to report higher levels of psychological stress?

  A. Specialised hospital unit.

  B. General hospital ward.

  C. Home.

  D. Hospice.

Your answer:

20. In which setting would you associate the phrase 'death with dignity'?

A. Home.

B. Specialised hospital ward.

C. Hospice care.

D. Intensive care ward.

Your answer: [ ]

21. Which of the following is not an example of mourning?

A. Wearing black to a funeral.

B. Intense psychological distress.

C. Closing the curtains when someone dies.

D. Conducting rituals.

Your answer: [ ]

22. Contemporary thought on the grieving process suggests which of the following?

A. Grieving is a stage-based process which occurs in a set sequence.

B. Individuals move back and forth between phases of grieving.

C. Grieving is better understood as a set of tasks.

D. Both B and C.

Your answer: [ ]

23. Audrey's husband George has recently passed away. George took care of all their financial business. Now Audrey must learn to take care of the finances. This is an example of what?

A. Avoidance.

B. Confrontation.

C. Restoration.

D. Anticipatory grieving.

Your answer: [ ]

24. Chitra and her husband lost their baby while Chitra was four months pregnant. Chitra blames herself and asks how it might have been prevented. This is an example of what?

A. Avoidance.

B. Confrontation.

C. Restoration.

D. Anticipatory grieving.

Your answer:

25. During confrontation, the grief stricken individual shows which of the following characteristics?

A. Lose their appetite, engage in self-destructive behaviours.

B. Overcome loneliness by reaching out to others.

C. Experience emotional anaesthesia.

D. Revise their identity.

Your answer:

26. The dual-process model emphasises that effective coping requires people to do what?

A. Forge a symbolic bond with the deceased.

B. Deal with the emotional consequences of loss before attending to life changes.

C. Deal with life changes before attending to the emotional consequences of loss.

D. Alternate between dealing with the emotional consequences of loss and attending to life changes.

Your answer:

27. Elizabeth's grandma is 94 and has advanced dementia. Elizabeth knows that her grandma does not have long to live and is trying to prepare herself for her inevitable death. Elizabeth is experiencing which of the following?

    A. Premature grieving.

    B. Anticipatory grieving.

    C. Prolonged grieving.

    D. Anticipatory mourning.

    Your answer: ☐

28. Which of the following is most likely to contribute to a child's ability to grieve?

    A. Stage of cognitive development.

    B. Honesty, affection and reassurance.

    C. Sudden as opposed to prolonged death.

    D. Both A and B.

    Your answer: ☐

29. Which of the following is not an example of how a child may cope with the death of a loved one?

    A. Dreaming about and speaking to them regularly.

    B. Re-establishing life's meaning through other activities.

    C. Believing that their loved one has left them voluntarily but will come back.

    D. Worrying that other people who they love may disappear too.

    Your answer: ☐

30. Over the past 12 months, Jane has lost three close family members. Jane may experience which of the following?

    A. Bereavement overload.

    B. Unanticipated mourning.

    C. Anticipatory grief.

    D. Dual grief.

    Your answer: ☐

Extended multiple-choice question

Complete the following paragraphs using the items listed below and opposite. Not all of the items will be needed and each item can only be used once.

The right to die is a topic of fierce ethical debate. _____, the practice of ending a person's life who is suffering from an incurable condition, can take various forms. The withholding of treatment at the patient's request is referred to as _____. Despite acceptance by the majority of individuals, some _____ have expressed concern that this form of euthanasia might represent a step towards _____. Another approach might be the administering of a lethal dose of drugs; this is known as active euthanasia and is carried out at the patient's request. _____ is an alternative form of euthanasia. For example, a doctor may enable the patient to swallow a lethal dose of drugs to end life. Voluntary active euthanasia has been suggested to be the most _____ way of ending life for those with terminal illness and is favoured over assisted suicide. However, all forms of euthanasia clearly possess profound _____ and _____ dilemmas.

Controversial court cases have led to the development of a number of methods to ensure the legal protection of doctors and healthcare professionals. These include an _____, a written statement of desired medical treatment should the patient become terminally ill, and a _____, a patient's preferences for the treatment that they want in the case of a terminal illness.

Optional items

A. advance medical directive

B. assisted suicide

C. compassionate

D. clinical

E. durable power of attorney

F. euthanasia

G. legal

H. living will

I. mercy killing

J. moral

K. passive euthanasia

L. religious communities

M. voluntary euthanasia

Essay questions for Chapter 11

Once you have completed the MCQs above you are ready to tackle some essay questions. You might like to select three or four topics and make notes on them. One way of doing this is to create a concept map. The first question has been done for you and you can see how the knowledge required links to some of the MCQs in this chapter.

1. With reference to adult psychosocial theories of development, discuss the extent to which death anxiety decreases with age.

2. Describe and evaluate Kübler-Ross's theory of the psychological needs of people who are dying.

3. Discuss the extent to which hospitals can meet the needs of those who are dying and their families.

4. Discuss the impact of hospice care on the quality of life of those who are dying.

5. Describe and evaluate the ethical implications of voluntary euthanasia and assisted suicide.

6. Evaluate the role of personal and situational factors in the grieving process.

7. Discuss factors that explain how children and adults may differ in grieving for a loved one.

8. Discuss how the dual-process model of coping with loss may enable individuals to cope with bereavement.

Chapter 11 essay question 1: concept map

With reference to adult psychosocial theories of development, discuss the extent to which death anxiety decreases with age.

The concept map below provides an example of the topic areas that you might include when writing your essay. Remember that it is important to link your answers to other topic areas not covered in this chapter. This question requires you to describe and evaluate the extent to which death anxiety declines with age. Good answers to this question will consider cultural variations of death anxiety in addition to gender differences. It is also important that you draw on theories of adult psychosocial development to support your answer, but maintaining a critical evaluative perspective.

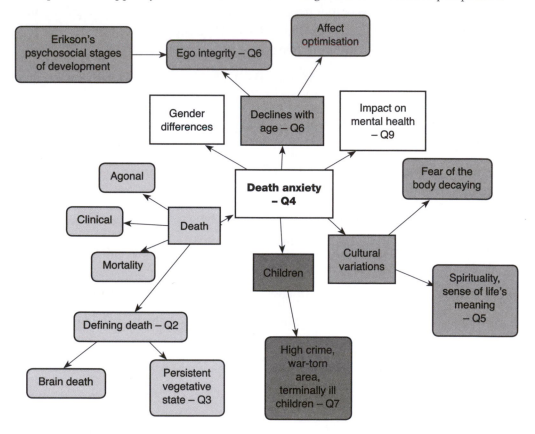

Writing an essay: a format for success

Writing a good essay is an essential skill that you will need to develop during your degree, whatever the topic may be. Below are some general tips on how to write a good essay. These can be used to help you with any essay topic that you may encounter throughout your degree, not just those written in this book.

Getting started

Good preparation and planning are essential to effective essay writing. Before you put pen to paper, you should ensure that you have researched your topic thoroughly and gathered information from a range of sources, e.g. journal articles, books, websites, etc. Creating a concept map similar to those within this book may also help you organise your thoughts and provide structure to your essay. Remember that writing a good essay is as much about style as content. Your essay should be clearly written and develop a convincing argument.

Structuring your essay

A good essay will consist of three parts: an introduction, the main argument and a conclusion.

- In the introduction you should begin by writing a brief statement to introduce the topic. This is usually the most difficult part of writing an essay but do not spend too long trying to write a brilliant opening sentence, you can always return to this later. You should then outline how you propose to answer the question set and define any key terms. You should assume that the reader of your essay has no prior knowledge of your essay topic. The length of your introduction will depend on the word limit but make sure you do not spend the best part of your essay explaining how you will answer the question.

- The next section will consist of your main argument. This should follow the same sequence that you outlined in your introduction. In answering any essay question, it is important that your argument is evidence based. In other words, do not make any sweeping statements that cannot be backed up with evidence from the literature. In order to achieve the higher grades it is essential that your essay is not just descriptive but also takes a critical and evaluative stance. To do this you need to think about the advantages and disadvantages of the theories and research that you discuss in your essay and not take the evidence at face value.

- The conclusion of your essay should bring together the points that you have made throughout your essay and enable you to develop an informed decision. It is also an opportunity for you to present an original stance on your topic.

- Finally, make sure that you have actually answered the question that you set out to answer. Proofreading your essay is one way to do this.

- You will also need to compile a reference list. This will include every source that you have cited throughout your essay. All references should be written in the style of the American Psychological Association (APA). If you are not sure how to format your reference list, check your course handbook or contact your module leader. Alternatively there are many websites that provide examples of how to cite various sources using APA. The Owl at Purdue is a good resource and can be accessed using the web link: http://owl.english.purdue.edu/owl/resource/560/01/.

Scoring methods in MCQs

Introduction

All assessments need to be reviewed and marked. At your university you will come across a number of formal (often called summative) and informal (aka formative) assessments. These can take the form of practical reports, essays, short-answer questions and (of course) examinations. There are, of course, a number of forms of examinations – short answers, written essays and multiple-choice questions (or MCQs).

MCQs are considered objective assessments, that is answers are unambiguously correct or incorrect and therefore provide for high marker reliability – so that's one positive mark for MCQs. On the other hand, there is often a concern (for the examination setter) that guessing by the candidate can have an inflationary influence on the marks. By chance, if you have four choices then you should score 25% just by guessing. This is obviously not a situation to be encouraged, and because of this your psychology course team may have introduced various attempts to make sure that this does not happen. It is worth exploring some of these methods and the implications these will have for the approach you take to your assessment and, ultimately, how they can impact on your examination performance.

Scoring of MCQ examinations can take several forms. At its most simple, a raw score is calculated based on the total number of correct responses (usually 1 mark per correct answer). Under this approach, any omissions or incorrect responses earn you no marks but neither do they attract a penalty. If you get the question right, you get a mark; if you do not then you get no mark.

As mentioned, alternative and more complex approaches to marking have been developed because of concerns that results can be inflated if correct responses are the result of successful guessing. The most common approaches to discouraging random guessing include the reward of partial knowledge and negative marking. This can impact on your behaviour and your learning. Of course, whatever the examination and whatever the marking scheme, you need to know your stuff!

Rewarding partial knowledge

Scoring procedures developed to reward partial knowledge are based on the assumption that though you and your student colleagues may be unable to identify a single correct response you can confidently identify some options as being incorrect and that partial knowledge should therefore be rewarded. Versions of this approach generally allow you to choose:

- more than one possibly correct response and to be awarded a partial mark provided one of your responses is the correct answer;
- a 'not sure' option for which you are awarded a proportion of a mark (usually either 0.2 or 0.25).

Negative marking

Negative marking is when your performance is based on the total number of correct responses which is then reduced in some way to correct for any potential guessing. The simplest application of negative marking is where equal numbers of marks are added or subtracted for right and wrong answers and omitted answers or the selection of a 'No answer' option that has no impact on marks. So, you get +1 mark when you get the question right, –1 mark when you get it wrong and 0 if you do not attempt it. However, there are other approaches which are slightly more punitive. In these approaches, if you get the question correct you get +1, if you get the question wrong then this is awarded a –1 (or even –2) and if there is no attempt then this is awarded a –1 as well as, it is suggested, you do not know the answer.

How does this impact on you?

The impact of these scoring mechanisms can be significant. By way of example, use the following table to demonstrate your performance in each of the chapters in this text. For each of the chapters work out the number of correct responses (and code this as NC), the number of incorrect answers (coded as NI) and the number of questions that you did not provide a response to (NR). You can then use the formulae in the table to work out how you would have performed under each of the different marking schemes. For example, for the punitive negative marking scheme you score 18 correct (NC=18), 2 incorrect (NI=2) and omitted 5 questions (NR=5). On the basis of the formula in the table, NC-(NI*2)-NR, you would have scored 9 (i.e. 18-(2*2)-5). So even though you managed to get 18 out of 25 this would have been reduced to only 9 because of the punitive marking.

Chapter	Number correct	Number incorrect	No response	Marking scheme: raw score	Marking scheme: partial knowledge	Marking scheme: negative marking	Marking scheme: punitive negative marking
	NC	NI	NR	= NC	= NC − (NI * 0.2)	= NC − NI	= NC − (NI * 2) − NR
1							
2							
3							
4							
5							
6							
7							
8							
9							
10							
11							
TOTAL							

Explore the scores above – which chapter did you excel at and for which chapter do you need to do some work? Use the above table to see your areas of strength and areas of weakness – and consequently where you need to spend more time revising and reviewing the material.

MCQ answers

Chapter 1: Themes, theories and key figures in developmental psychology – MCQ answers

Level	Question number	Correct response	Self-monitoring
Foundation	1	B	
Foundation	2	B	
Foundation	3	C	
Foundation	4	B	
Foundation	5	C	
Foundation	6	B	
Foundation	7	D	
Foundation	8	C	
Foundation	9	A	
Foundation	10	C	
Advanced	11	B	
Advanced	12	D	
Advanced	13	A	
Advanced	14	D	
Advanced	15	A	
Advanced	16	B	
Advanced	17	D	
Advanced	18	D	
Advanced	19	D	
Advanced	20	A	
		Total number of points:	Foundation: Advanced:

EMCQ for Chapter 1

The paragraphs should read as follows. A maximum of 11 points can be allocated.

The nature versus nurture or the <u>heredity</u> versus <u>environment</u> argument is one of the most controversial debates in the history of psychology. Contemporary thought emphasises an interaction between genes and environmental influences. <u>Armstrong (2007)</u> suggested that neurological and psychological functions are intrinsically linked to each other: one drives the development of the other therefore it is impossible to differentiate the two. As a result, researchers have now questioned the extent to which this occurs by investigating how much of the <u>variance</u> can be explained by genetics and how genetics and the environment interact. Variance is measured by <u>heritability estimates</u> obtained from kinship studies which compare the characteristics of family members, for example intelligence. However, this provides no indication of how intelligence develops and ignores the context in which development occurs. <u>Reaction range</u> and <u>genetic-environmental correlations</u> are two methods that have attempted to explain how genetics and the environment impact upon development and emphasise the idea that development is affected by <u>multiple interacting forces</u>.

<u>Bronfenbrenner</u> suggests that development is additionally affected by <u>proximal processes</u>, the number of enduring relationships and activities that the person has in their immediate environment. Heredity estimates only tell us what the environment is bringing to fruition, the non-realised <u>genetic potential</u> remains unknown. In other words, it is not possible to determine the extent to which development is influenced by genetics and the environment.

Chapter 2: Prenatal development and birth – MCQ answers

Level	Question number	Correct response	Self-monitoring
Foundation	1	B	
Foundation	2	C	
Foundation	3	A	
Foundation	4	D	
Foundation	5	A	
Foundation	6	B	
Foundation	7	D	
Foundation	8	A	
Foundation	9	D	
Foundation	10	A	
Advanced	11	B	
Advanced	12	D	
Advanced	13	B	
Advanced	14	D	
Advanced	15	A	
Advanced	16	B	
Advanced	17	C	
Advanced	18	B	
Advanced	19	A	
Advanced	20	A	
		Total number of points:	Foundation: Advanced:

EMCQ for Chapter 2

The correct statements are as follows. A maximum of 5 points can be awarded.

A. Low income.

D. Poor education.

G. Living in a deprived area.

I. Lack of support lack from family members.

J. Limited access to good prenatal care.

Chapter 3: Motor and perceptual development – MCQ answers

Level	Question number	Correct response	Self-monitoring
Foundation	1	A	
Foundation	2	C	
Foundation	3	A	
Foundation	4	B	
Foundation	5	D	
Foundation	6	A	
Foundation	7	C	
Foundation	8	B	
Foundation	9	C	
Foundation	10	C	
Foundation	11	C	
Foundation	12	B	
Foundation	13	D	
Advanced	14	C	
Advanced	15	D	
Advanced	16	A	
Advanced	17	C	
Advanced	18	B	
Advanced	19	C	
Advanced	20	A	
Advanced	21	B	
Advanced	22	D	
Advanced	23	C	
Advanced	24	A	
Advanced	25	A	
Advanced	26	B	
		Total number of points:	Foundation: Advanced:

EMCQ for Chapter 3

The table should be completed as follows. A maximum of 10 points can be awarded.

Motor skill	Average age achieved
Holds head upright	6 weeks
Rolls from side to back	2 months
Grasps a block	3 months
Sits without support	7 months
Plays pat-a-cake	9 months
Stands without support	11 months
Walks without support	12 months
Scribbles	14 months
Jumps in place	23 months
Walks on tiptoe	25 months

Chapter 4: Attachment – MCQ answers

Level	Question number	Correct response	Self-monitoring
Foundation	1	C	
Foundation	2	A	
Foundation	3	A	
Foundation	4	B	
Foundation	5	A	
Foundation	6	D	
Foundation	7	C	
Foundation	8	B	
Foundation	9	C	
Foundation	10	D	
Foundation	11	A	
Foundation	12	B	
Foundation	13	C	
Advanced	14	D	
Advanced	15	A	
Advanced	16	B	
Advanced	17	D	
Advanced	18	A	
Advanced	19	C	
Advanced	20	B	
Advanced	21	D	
Advanced	22	A	
Advanced	23	A	
Advanced	24	A	
Advanced	25	C	
Advanced	26	D	
		Total number of points:	Foundation: Advanced:

EMCQ for Chapter 4

The paragraph should read as follows. A maximum of 11 points can be awarded.

Attachment theorists including <u>Bowlby</u> have suggested that the quality of an infant's attachment to their caregiver has salient consequences for later development. Infants who establish <u>secure attachments</u> should develop into confident children who are able to form good relationships with their peers. For example, <u>Matas et al. (1978)</u> found that securely attached children were more enthusiastic, frustrated less easily and were more persistent in finding a solution to a problem-solving task than <u>insecurely</u> attached infants when observed at 18 and 24 months of age. This suggests that early <u>social experiences</u> have a profound effect on later social, emotional and cognitive development. However, longitudinal research has found that this is not always the case. Consequently, <u>continuity</u> of caregiving has been identified as a factor that may determine whether <u>attachment security</u> is maintained in later development. Initial security of attachment in infancy provides a good starting point for a positive parent–child relationship; however, this is <u>conditional</u> upon the quality of the child's future relationships. This indicates that attachment is not always <u>stable</u> over time and highlights the <u>bi-directional</u> relationship between parent and child in the development of attachment.

Chapter 5: Language development – MCQ answers

Level	Question number	Correct response	Self-monitoring
Foundation	1	B	
Foundation	2	B	
Foundation	3	A	
Foundation	4	A	
Foundation	5	C	
Foundation	6	D	
Foundation	7	B	
Foundation	8	D	
Foundation	9	A	
Foundation	10	C	
Foundation	11	D	
Foundation	12	C	
Advanced	13	A	
Advanced	14	B	
Advanced	15	B	
Advanced	16	D	
Advanced	17	A	
Advanced	18	C	
Advanced	19	B	
Advanced	20	C	
Advanced	21	A	
Advanced	22	B	
Advanced	23	D	
Advanced	24	A	
		Total number of points:	Foundation: Advanced:

EMCQ for Chapter 5

The paragraph should read as follows. A maximum of 10 points can be awarded.

<u>Bilingualism</u> is the ability to learn <u>two</u> languages at a time. Children can become bilingual by either acquiring both languages at the same time during <u>early</u> childhood or <u>learning</u> a second language after the first. Learning a second language in childhood is often <u>easier</u> than learning later in life. This is because a <u>sensitive</u> period exists for language mastery. The ability to learn an additional language is thought to decrease in a <u>continuous</u> and <u>age-related</u> way from childhood to adulthood but no specific age for decline in language learning ability has been identified. Research evidence has suggested that bilingual children often do better on tests of <u>selective attention</u> and <u>cognitive flexibility</u>. They may also have a greater awareness of grammatical errors, or <u>metalinguistic awareness</u>.

Chapter 6: Play and peer interaction – MCQ answers

Level	Question number	Correct response	Self-monitoring
Foundation	1	B	
Foundation	2	D	
Foundation	3	B	
Foundation	4	A	
Foundation	5	A	
Foundation	6	B	
Foundation	7	D	
Foundation	8	B	
Foundation	9	D	
Foundation	10	A	
Advanced	11	C	
Advanced	12	C	
Advanced	13	B	
Advanced	14	A	
Advanced	15	A	
Advanced	16	D	
Advanced	17	D	
Advanced	18	A	
Advanced	19	C	
Advanced	20	C	
		Total number of points:	Foundation: Advanced:

EMCQ for Chapter 6

The paragraph should read as follows. A maximum of 10 points can be awarded.

Friendship can be defined as a relationship between two or more individuals that requires commitment and <u>reciprocity</u>. <u>Gottman (1983)</u> tape-recorded conversations of children and identified <u>six</u> processes involved in friendship formation that distinguished play patterns of children with their best friends compared to with strangers. He also suggested that the focus of friendship is thought to change with age. In early childhood, the goal of peer interaction is to achieve <u>coordinated play</u> whereas older children are more concerned with <u>peer acceptance</u> and <u>rejection</u>. In adolescence the focus of friendship is much more on <u>self-disclosure</u>. Sullivan (1953) suggested that friendship serves a number of functions, for example to provide affection and promote the growth of <u>interpersonal sensitivity</u>. Rubin and Coplan (1992) suggest additional functions of friendship including providing a context for transmitting <u>social norms</u>. Friendships have also been argued to offer a <u>secure base</u> outside of the family setting.

Chapter 7: Cognitive development – MCQ answers

Level	Question number	Correct response	Self-monitoring
Foundation	1	C	
Foundation	2	A	
Foundation	3	B	
Foundation	4	D	
Foundation	5	B	
Foundation	6	A	
Foundation	7	A	
Foundation	8	D	
Foundation	9	C	
Foundation	10	D	
Foundation	11	B	
Foundation	12	B	
Foundation	13	C	
Foundation	14	A	
Advanced	15	A	
Advanced	16	B	
Advanced	17	C	
Advanced	18	D	
Advanced	19	B	
Advanced	20	A	
Advanced	21	D	
Advanced	22	B	
Advanced	23	D	
Advanced	24	B	
Advanced	25	C	
Advanced	26	B	
Advanced	27	B	
Advanced	28	A	
		Total number of points:	Foundation: Advanced:

EMCQ for Chapter 7

The paragraph should read as follows. A maximum of 13 points can be awarded.

The <u>information processing approach</u> views cognitive development as an analogy between the computer and the human mind. Information processing theories share three basic assumptions. The first is that <u>thought processes</u> such as <u>remembering</u> are a form of information processing. Secondly, information processing theories emphasise <u>change mechanisms</u> that move development from one state to the next. The third assumption is <u>self-modification</u>, the idea that previous knowledge can modify thinking and facilitate higher levels of cognitive development. Siegler (1998) suggested that information processing theories emphasise the <u>structural characteristics</u> and <u>processes</u> that provide mechanisms for the adaptation of cognition to environmental influences. These structural characteristics include stores such as a <u>sensory register</u>, <u>working memory</u> and <u>long-term memory</u>. Processes include <u>encoding</u> and <u>automisation</u>. More recently, information processing research has expanded to include <u>developmental cognitive neuroscience</u> incorporating psychology, biology, neuroscience and medicine to advance our understanding of the relationship between changes in the brain, cognitive processing and behaviour.

Chapter 8: Moral development – MCQ answers

Level	Question number	Correct response	Self-monitoring
Foundation	1	B	
Foundation	2	C	
Foundation	3	A	
Foundation	4	D	
Foundation	5	B	
Foundation	6	A	
Foundation	7	C	
Foundation	8	C	
Foundation	9	A	
Foundation	10	D	
Foundation	11	A	
Foundation	12	B	
Advanced	13	B	
Advanced	14	A	
Advanced	15	B	
Advanced	16	C	
Advanced	17	D	
Advanced	18	A	
Advanced	19	C	
Advanced	20	B	
Advanced	21	B	
Advanced	22	A	
Advanced	23	D	
Advanced	24	D	
		Total number of points:	Foundation: Advanced:

EMCQ for Chapter 8

The paragraph should read as follows. A maximum of 10 points can be awarded.

Research has indicated that <u>emotion</u> also plays an important role in moral development, specifically in moral behaviour. Emotions such as gratitude, guilt and love can mediate the <u>relationship</u> between moral thought and behaviour. Moral action can be expressed through <u>prosocial behaviour</u> while immoral action can typically involve <u>aggression</u>. Gains in prosocial behaviour have been attributed to changes in <u>cognitive development</u>, emotional understanding and the child's <u>environment</u>. Research examining the development of prosocial behaviour has identified that it is <u>stable</u> over time; children who are kind and considerate at <u>age 7</u> are likely to remain so at <u>age 14</u>. Consequently, behaviour in early childhood is regarded as a strong predictor of behaviour in later development. Evidence from <u>twin studies</u> has highlighted the role of genes in the development of prosocial behaviour; however, the contribution of <u>environmental factors</u> is also important.

Chapter 9: Identity development – MCQ answers

Level	Question number	Correct response	Self-monitoring
Foundation	1	A	
Foundation	2	C	
Foundation	3	A	
Foundation	4	D	
Foundation	5	B	
Foundation	6	C	
Foundation	7	C	
Foundation	8	B	
Foundation	9	C	
Foundation	10	A	
Foundation	11	B	
Foundation	12	A	
Foundation	13	C	
Foundation	14	B	
Foundation	15	A	
Advanced	16	D	
Advanced	17	D	
Advanced	18	B	
Advanced	19	C	
Advanced	20	B	
Advanced	21	D	
Advanced	22	A	
Advanced	23	A	
Advanced	24	B	
Advanced	25	A	
Advanced	26	D	
Advanced	27	C	
Advanced	28	B	
Advanced	29	A	
Advanced	30	D	
		Total number of points:	Foundation: Advanced:

EMCQ for Chapter 9

The paragraphs should read as follows. A maximum of 11 points can be awarded.

In 1904 G. Stanley Hall proposed that adolescence is essentially a period of storm and stress, a period of psychological turmoil. This comprised three specific characteristics: mood disruption, conflict with parents and engagement in risk-taking behaviours. Hall adopted a Lamarckian evolutionary perspective suggesting that evolution occurs when organisms pass on their characteristics from one generation to the next, not in the form of genes but in the form of experiences and acquired characteristics.

However, Margaret Mead (1928) argued that not all groups will show signs of a 'tumultuous' period; rather it represents a gradual transition from childhood to adolescence. Arnett proposed that not all adolescents experience storm and stress; rather, adolescence is a period when storm and stress is more likely to occur. Parental warmth, conflict and establishing autonomy are vital factors in emotional development; absence of parental warmth, whether physical or verbal, may result in symptoms of storm and stress. The rise of globalisation is also thought to be a contributing factor.

Chapter 10: Adulthood – MCQ answers

Level	Question number	Correct response	Self-monitoring
Foundation	1	A	
Foundation	2	B	
Foundation	3	C	
Foundation	4	A	
Foundation	5	D	
Foundation	6	B	
Foundation	7	C	
Foundation	8	D	
Foundation	9	A	
Foundation	10	C	
Foundation	11	B	
Foundation	12	A	
Foundation	13	B	
Foundation	14	C	
Foundation	15	D	
Advanced	16	C	
Advanced	17	B	
Advanced	18	A	
Advanced	19	D	
Advanced	20	C	
Advanced	21	D	
Advanced	22	C	
Advanced	23	B	
Advanced	24	A	
Advanced	25	C	
Advanced	26	D	
Advanced	27	A	
Advanced	28	D	
Advanced	29	B	
Advanced	30	B	
		Total number of points:	Foundation: Advanced:

EMCQ for Chapter 10

The table should be completed as follows. A maximum of 10 points can be awarded.

Retire	Continue working
Good pension	Flexible working
Financially secure	Rewarding job
Health problems	Stimulating work environment
Reached highest point in profession	
Spend more time on the golf course	
Spend more time with the grandchildren	
Spouse due to retire	

Chapter 11: Death, dying and bereavement – MCQ answers

Level	Question number	Correct response	Self-monitoring
Foundation	1	C	
Foundation	2	B	
Foundation	3	C	
Foundation	4	D	
Foundation	5	B	
Foundation	6	D	
Foundation	7	D	
Foundation	8	A	
Foundation	9	B	
Foundation	10	D	
Foundation	11	A	
Foundation	12	C	
Foundation	13	B	
Foundation	14	D	
Foundation	15	C	
Advanced	16	D	
Advanced	17	B	
Advanced	18	A	
Advanced	19	C	
Advanced	20	C	
Advanced	21	B	
Advanced	22	D	
Advanced	23	C	
Advanced	24	B	
Advanced	25	A	
Advanced	26	D	
Advanced	27	B	
Advanced	28	D	
Advanced	29	B	
Advanced	30	A	
		Total number of points:	Foundation: Advanced:

EMCQ for Chapter 11

The paragraphs should read as follows. A maximum of 10 points can be awarded.

The right to die is a topic of fierce ethical debate. <u>Euthanasia,</u> the practice of ending a person's life who is suffering from an incurable condition, can take various forms. The withholding of treatment at the patient's request is referred to as <u>passive euthanasia.</u> Despite acceptance by the majority of individuals, some <u>religious communities</u> have expressed concern that this form of euthanasia might represent a step towards <u>mercy killing.</u> Another approach might be the administering of a lethal dose of drugs; this is known as active euthanasia and is carried out at the patient's request. <u>Assisted suicide</u> is an alternative form of euthanasia. For example, a doctor may enable the patient to swallow a lethal dose of drugs to end life. Voluntary active euthanasia has been suggested to be the most <u>compassionate</u> way of ending life for those with terminal illness and is favoured over assisted suicide. However, all forms of euthanasia clearly possess profound <u>moral</u> and <u>legal</u> dilemmas.

Controversial court cases have led to the development of a number of methods to ensure the legal protection of doctors and healthcare professionals. These include an <u>advance medical directive,</u> a written statement of desired medical treatment should the patient become terminally ill, and a <u>living will,</u> a patient's preferences for the treatment that they want in the case of a terminal illness.